TWEEKER

Works by Luis Blasini

BORROWED FLESH
TWEEKER
CLASS CONSCIOUS POETRY
PUTA
DARK IS THE NIGHT
OF MEN AND MAGGOTS
HOBOSEXUAL
TIJUANA BEBOP
BLEW THE SHOT
ACROSS THE GALACTIC LENS
THE WARLORDS OF JUPITER

TWEEKER

a novel by
Luis Blasini

Five Fingered Press
New York

Published by Five Fingered Press, 2009

Printed in the United States of America

Library of Congress Cataloging-in-Publication Data

Blasini, Luis, 1967—

Tweeker / by Luis Blasini---1st U.S. ed. P. cm.

ISBN 9781441489036

1.Novelists, American - Biography. 2. Drug Addicts - United States. 3. Mental Health - United States - Biography. 4. Homosexuality.

I. Title

"Tweeker. The term coined for the sleep deprivation crystal meth addicts usually undergo. Some user would stay up for two weeks at a time, so came the phrase 'two-weeker' which eventually became tweeker. Like, it's been days since that guy's gotten any sleep or had something to eat. He's gotta be a tweeker."

- Anonymous addict

I GLANCED from my beer glass towards the muck splattered, concrete stairs which led up to the street. The small cantina, in which I sat, was a hazy, dank room. It held the smell of fresh rain and backed up toilets.

Within the dim saloon lay a scuffed, green-velvet pool table, a warped counter of decaying mahogany lined with a row of wobbly, aluminum-tubed stools occupied with sulky drunks who sat staring sullenly into their drinks. Plastered on the dark, stained walls were garish Lucha libre posters which curled at the torn corners. The only color illuminating the room was from a string of red Christmas lights which sagged at one end over the bar.

An obscene, flesh-colored, rubber dildo – smeared in grime and verdigris - attached to a pair of dingy, pink panties sat in a dusty cubbyhole on the wall behind the register.

Underneath, a crudely scrawled sign in Spanish read, *ARE THESE YOURS?*

Outside the lonely bar, rain cascaded in black, shimmering sheets in a vain attempt to wash away all the evil and filth of the city that dismal, lonely night.

On street level, the border town of Tijuana sprawled in the battering torrents like an old and bloated Mexican whore, wallowing and screaming in drunken fits of intoxicated, excessive debauchery.

Across her muck-splattered carcass, a selection of mariachi music clashed with the mosaic neon of discos thumping hip-hop nonsense toward loud, vomiting American tourists. Sad-eyed prostitutes lurked against dirty, white-washed adobe walls with their come-on looks beckoning despondently at stumbling and intoxicated clients. The whores grabbed at the pale arms as they passed, needle tracks dreamily fade into smooth, copper flesh with faint, blue incandescence.

On this wet night, police slouched on every corner; waiting to shoot somebody or do anything other than stand there under hostile eyes of both wet, bewildered tourists and calculating, local con-men who rapidly darted over fluorescent pools of soggy garbage.

Beneath that never-ending carnival of filth, I sat at the bar, hunched on the padded stool, experiencing the slow gravity pull of time.

Half a cigarette later, I peered toward my left: a withered and ancient fucker in a faded Stetson silently scrutinized me through squinted, blood-shot eyes.

He curtly saluted with two, pudgy fingers; mouth a black, toothless hole, *"Hola!"*

I silently returned to my beer.

Time passed.

I flicked a small, brown cockroach off the bar counter into an ice bin that held the beer bottles. Yawn. I took out a crumpled packet of cigarettes - lit one. Through grey smoke, I gazed at the clock. He was late.

Cigarette - cigarette - cigarette.

A shadowy figure slopped down the stairs and shuffled into the cantina – tennis shoes squished loudly, leaving slime pools on the dirty, red-checkered tile.

Long, wet, obsidian hair covered his face. A brown, square jaw jutted from beneath the shiny mane. He wore a ratty, black denim jacket, black *Metallica* t-shirt, and jeans. His soaked attire was well-worn and grimy mud was splattered up the lower legs.

We both mumbled *whutsup* and he ordered a beer. Red-tinted eyes of amber sparkled past the shock of limp, black hair which cascaded over Aztec Indian features. An expression of intense hostility emitted from that visage – a smooth face both brutal and handsome. From a short, thin torso, he imparted a cocky, street-wise, macho insolence which portrayed an older persona – far older than his actual twenty-one years revealed.

Casually, he took a puff from my cigarette and asked through silver-capped teeth, "You ready to go?" The voice was nasal and forced like the squeak of a wounded rodent.

"Let's get the fuck outta here." I coughed, squishing the cigarette out into an ashtray on the counter.

We went up and out into the rain. Sheets of the shit straight from some Mickey Spillane pulp illuminated with the passing searchlights of prowling kamikaze taxis, the two of us dashed over incandescent pools and muddy rivers of gurgling sewage. Passing through long shadows, we quickly strode the murky blocks to a windowless, adobe building with a red-painted steel door.

The two of us stood in the downpour as my spectral friend put his thick lips up to a small, rectangular hole cut into the door, *"Coo-coo Coo-coo!"*

He repeated the call three times.

With a series of sharp, metal clangs, the door was opened by a young fag in a Marine fatigue hat - tall and thin in tight, grey jeans and an olive, denim jacket. His attractive face, smooth and possessing aquiline features, displayed a supple mouth, and doe-like eyes. He stood a moment and glared at us with paranoid mistrust.

"Que quieres, Mario?" The fag bitchily spat.

Mario mumbled something in Spanish.

The fag's prissy demeanor dissolved as he coyly smiled at me, *"Pásale."*

The high ceilinged, white-washed foyer was darkly lit with flickering candles. In a corner on a plastic milk crate sat a plump, archaic mamacita in a red-flowered smock. She nonchalantly picked through a porcelain bowl of frijoles under a multi-hued mosaic of Guadalupe.

"Buenas noches." She creaked from a round, prunish face.

Mario and I repeated the greeting as we followed the fag down a long, dank maze of halls bearing the overpowering smell of mildew and clogged toilets; eventually entering a large, faintly lit room occupied with a gathering of about ten to fifteen Mexicans.

In the dim light, the throng stood or milled about with red, plastic cups in hand as a multi-speaker stereo blasted high-decimal ranchero music. Hipsters to be sure, the party guests were a mix of young and old working class in dark, damp clothes. The shadowy din resonated with festive laughter and chattering conversations.

Mario asked me to wait as he and the fag slinked into the smokey gloom. Left alone at the room's entrance, I looked down at a grey chicken pecking next to my feet. To my right was a set of dilapidated French doors that opened to an outside patio – the continuing rain was a hue of dull yellow from the ambient light which filtered from the room.

Two locals approached me from a nearby group. One held out and offered an extra cup of beer.

"Hey, *guero*, what's up?" The tall, skinny one asked. He brandished a tattoo of two teardrops below the right, thick-lashed eye. He was attractive with shabby street clothes and shaved head.

The shorter, frog-faced Indian smiled, "Who did you come with?"

I took the beer and pointed into the murk, "A friend. He's over there."

They both glanced over and spotted Mario in an animated discussion with an old, skeletal phantom wearing a damp trench coat, green Russian military cap, and black, wrap-around shades.

"*Oh, con Mario.*" The tall one smiled knowingly. "Are you from San Diego?" He then casually asked for a cigarette.

I passed him one of my smokes, "No, I live in Tijuana."

He fished a match out of his pocket and lit it with dirty fingernails.

"For reals?" The tall one grinned, incredulously. "You work in San Diego and live here, *verdad?*" He took a sip of his beer and asked what I did for a living.

"I don't work, per se. I'm more interested in writing reports for the citizens of the United

States." I droned esoterically. It was a vain attempt to come across as literate and worldly. It didn't.

The remark fell irrelevant on dulled, ignorant faces.

"You *federale*? You look like a cop." The short one asked with a menacing smile.

"I get that." I croaked. "A lot."

The tall one put a lean, brown finger up to my lips and smiled, "Loose lips sink ships 'round here." He smirked a macho smirk. "Don't worry - later you get your cookies, *guero*."

I grinned back. Was this charming thief coming on to me? Without a parting word, the two faded back into the crowd.

The fiesta continued. Reggaetón blared as inebriated cha-cha girls gyrated lasciviously with pachucos in hip-hop gear and the exuberant crowd downed caguama after caguama.

I caught snatches of dialogue concerning three metropolitan cops who were found the previous evening in a nearby street: decapitated, mutilated. Chuckles and sneers from the gossiping cluster. The lights played long, dark shadows on grimy walls as tattoo-covered gangsters slowly passed and gave me a suspicious eye.

Mario returned holding his leather belt in his hands and we both huddled in a corner, "Tie me up, *guero*."

I pulled up his sleeve and wrapped Mario's black and frayed belt around his left arm. Tightening it, I searched for a vein with shriveled, white fingers.

Mario produced a syringe and handed it to me. I slid the needle under his smooth, copper skin and up into a protruding vein. I pushed the plunger, watched with curious morbidity as the junk emptied into his body.

Momentarily, Mario's eyes slacked as he dreamily clawed at the belt with numbing fingers.

Leaning against the grey, crumbling wall, he passed me the syringe, "Wanna taste?"

I glanced off into the hazy room. Two, flabby Latina girls began dancing to salsa music in the middle of the bare concrete floor - the crowd festively clapped along.

Through the muddled darkness on the other side, I noticed the flick-flickering of lighters; the red cherries of stems. Patter of mumbling junkies:

"Toke that, *pendejo*..."

"You fucking tweeker, get the fuck out of the fucking window, they can fucking see you! *Fuck!*"

"Who got my lighter?!"

"No more...*no mas*..."

"Bitch! There was more in this sack! Where the fuck did my speed go?"

"Que quieres?!"

"What's in the bowl, bitch?!"

"Who's look'n?"

"Good ones."

"Quitters never win and tweekers never quit."

My glazed eyes snapped back into focus as the words echoed away into my head.

"Nah, Mario, I'll be right back," I said distractedly.

I left Mario to his mess and weaved across the room towards a smiling lesbian and a short, grinning Aztec Indian guy. They were holding a glass pipe.

When they noticed me shuffling up, they both stated, "*Bienvenidos*", offering the pipe.

Speed. Meth. Chalk. Ice. Crystal. Crank. Tweek. Glass. Those are but some of the various street names for methamphetamines.

Call it what you want. It all leads to the same insidious shit. Addiction.

Meth addiction is cunning as much as it is baffling. Speaking strictly from experience – it is not a nice drug. It is not even a particularly fun drug. Unless your idea of a good time is being wired to a teeth-grinding, trembling chucklehead for 48 hours, unable to sleep, while at the same time lashing out as a selfish, violent bastard to all and sundry.

For me, it began, like most people, as a casual and recreational thing to do. Before I knew it, my entire life became centered on the narcotic to the point where I couldn't imagine life without it. The sad part about speed is that the user never notices how messed up their lives become.

Back to the party in progress: I mumbled thank you, politely coughed, and took a hit. The euphoria began at my spine, rushing up across the back of my skull, and splashing to the forehead. My mind popped into the astute focus of all that was around me – every detail was lucidly amplified. A surge of adrenaline washed through my torso as my hands began to sweat. My breath quickened as all nerve centers throughout my body pleasantly lit up like a carnival marquee.

I pulled out a crumpled one-hundred peso note and casually handed it to the grinning lesbian.

"Okay...okay." She smiled big and friendly behind silver-capped teeth.

Time sped up, slowed down, sped up as I smoked my fill.

Pop. Crackle.

With concentrated jerks, I returned to Mario. On the nod, he leaned slumped against a grungy wall, strung out. One hand held up his pants, the other grasped the syringe. I gulped my beer, lit a cigarette, and inquired where the *baño* was.

"The green door." Someone answered.

Eventually, I found an old, wooden door painted avocado green. Opening it, I was met with a chunky girl squatting in front of a young cholo leaning against a rust-streaked, porcelain sink - she was sucking his cock. I mumbled *perdóname* and closed the door to wafts of marijuana smoke.

A trio of couples begun an obscene mambo bop in the middle of the large, smokey room as I attempted to locate another door to take a much-needed piss.

Out back on the wet, cobblestone patio, I approached two guys with their cocks out, urinating into the rain. I joined them. One was the tall pelon with the tear-drop tattoos.

"El journalista!" He smiled as water dripped down a lean face, catching on his pencil-thin mustache.

The other was the fag in the Marine cap.

"Hola, *guero!*" The fag said.

I was soon to find out that they were in the middle of sizing up each other's penis in the gloomy rain. I guess when you have to, you have to. I joined them and relieved my bladder.

"This way, guero." The fag said, smiling.

The fag coyly motioned us to follow him up rusted iron stairs that ran outside along the patio wall to a room with weather-beaten, French doors.

The cubicle was bare and lit by candlelight atop a dresser. Against a wall, there was an army cot and nails on the wall for jackets. A few moldy, stuffed animals adorned the cot. A large, glossy poster of a gyrating male pop star had been taped above the head of the bed.

Elongated shadows shimmied as I sat on a metal chair. The fag and the cholo took a seat on the bed.

The fag reached down toward the green-tiled floor and passed a half-empty bottle of Petron to the cholo. After taking a long slug, the cholo fumbled into his pant pocket and pulled out a joint, lit it.

The fag cooed with a fey side glance towards me, "Isn't he delicious? *Muy guapo.*"

In my current state, I glanced over the lithe, muscular frame of the cholo.

"Yeah", I grinned, taking another hit off of the joint. "I'd milk him like a cow every morning."

The two chuckled at the silly comment. Always I had found humor to be a powerful aphrodisiac.

"*Orale.*" The lanky pelon sighed as he leaned back on the bed with hands clasped behind his head. With a lurid smirk, he stated, "What to do? I am in a room with two, horny *jotos*...what to do?"

The fag noticed the same thing I did - the growing erection in the pelon's dark khakis.

The fag and I glanced at each other knowingly.

The cholo grinned, *"Porque no?"*

Indeed. Why not?

I nonchalantly unzipped the cholo's pants. The stiff penis was pulled out from said khakis as the fag and I took turns sucking on that lengthy, brown fucker.

Ultimately, the pelon sighed. He lifted his white t-shirt as globs of pearly semen spurted onto his flat stomach, matting the dark trail of thick hair which led from his belly button to his pubes.

I sat up and watched as the fag slurped and licked the remaining goo to the smirking satisfaction of the cholo. There was a moment of uncomfortable silence as the young man fastened his pants and stood up. He smoothed out the front of his khakis and gave the fag a curt nod. Before he bolted out the door and into the gloom, the pelon hit me up for fifty pesos.

"Why not?" I smiled as I slapped the bill into his hand.

The cholo mumbled adios or something equivalent and returned to the party.

The fag and I - Ismael, he said his name was - sat and talked, smoking weed and finishing off the bottle of tequila.

"You like the crystal?" He inquired in his Pidgeon English as he looked with concern into my ping-ponging eyes.

"No, not particularly."

"Then why do you do it? It is so bad."

I whispered grimly, "I don't know."

I honestly didn't. Self-destructive, I guess? Or a multitude of other meaningless reasons thought up by caseworkers of therapists which, in the end result, don't mean shit. Nevertheless, was anything self-destructive when done in moderation? I think not.

Ismael rose, flicked a dial, and played solemn jazz sax on a little, ratty radio. He then lay next to me on his side; hand on my leg, and casually asked, "I am so hot, *guero*. You wanna fuck me?"

He leered up at me with that detestable countenance only over-heated homosexuals could accomplish. A look of both perverse want and despairing guilt. It was ghastly.

I took a puff of my cigarette, "Uhm...no. No. You are nice – however, I gotta get back downstairs. I came with a friend and he's utterly lost without me."

I stood up - his hand slithered off my thigh. I opened the door.

"You seem kind of lost yourself," Ismael stated with a worried, sincere expression.

I mumbled thanks and walked out into the black storm.

2

The rain came down in hissing sheets. It was the middle of the night. Yellow glares of lamplight flared through the droplets which splashed upon empty, gloomy streets. There were no cars, no people out this night.

Huddled in between two vacant warehouses - as if attempting to shield itself from the downpour - squat the Rialto Theater, one of the last adult cinemas in downtown San Diego.

In 1970s pimp font, the fading words *Rialto Theater* hummed in a blue neon glow. The marquee - rusted from years of weathering the elements and ringed with burnt, sad, worn-out bulbs - buzzed loudly in the muted fizzing of the rainy night; barely lighting the red-brick building of the degenerate cinema.

Inside, coffee-colored water dripped from the leaking ceiling. Dark, rose-colored halls vibrated with the gasps and grunts of random, broken lust from a porno video projected onto a huge, soiled movie screen. The pornography illuminated the fifty or so theater seats in an other-worldly, azure glow.

With stern faces blank, lifeless, dead - the way faces of men always seemed to be when viewing pornography - the ten or so patrons gazed catatonic on a blonde cooze who screeched in a crack-induced frenzy. A tired, middle-aged jock pumped her million-dollar snatch with weary apathy.

Every few seconds, nestled down in the dim and iridescent blue of the audience seats, there would be a flick of a lighter followed by the red glow of a glass pipe from over half of the attending customers. Mixed with random coughs and slurps of sordid, decadent activities, the small cinema was hazy-grey with the wafting vapors of exhaled cigarette or methamphetamine smoke.

At the building's entrance, I sat in a small, oblong office and listened to the whispers of the rain outside attempting to drown the phantom moaning crackling over the speakers from the theater.

The dusty box office was cluttered with stacked porno cassette boxes, discarded video machines, and packs of concession supplies.

With two television monitors on a table, a filing cabinet, and a foul reclining chair which took up most of the space, there barely was enough room to maneuver from the box office window to the exit door which doubled as a concession stand.

I sat slumped in an office chair at the window with my feet propped up. A spiral notebook resting on my lap, I put pen to paper and attempted to knock out a corny science fiction story that mixed Buck Rogers with Chinese Kung Fu movies. *Colt Corrigan across the Galactic Lens* was the title.

Pensively wiping sweaty grime from the nosepiece of my black, horned-rim glasses, I inwardly agreed how cliché the title must sound. It was perfect.

I readjusted my glasses and focused my eyes on scuffed, thin-soled shoes. They stuck out from dirty jeans which hadn't been washed in weeks. My sweat-stained t-shirt (It used to be white, now a faded yellow) was covered by a cracked, black leather jacket. My father - a fag hating, wife-beating bastard in his own right - referred to my usual attire as: "The uniform of the obvious homosexual."

With the calming hiss of the rain outside, I reminisced on how I had been employed at this filthy, foul-smelling theater for the past six months. On the merits of working the box-office graveyard shift in a rundown porno theater and how it could ebb away the old ego. Mostly dwelling on how I unconditionally loathed it.

What the fuck was I thinking when I took this stupid ass job? Summed up my dismay.

Nonetheless, there were certain perks. For example, the nightly comedy from a random junkie creep who, after over dramatically recoiling at the six dollar price of admission, would eagerly pay with a bump of meth to enter them pearly gates. Wherein, he realized one could hold up in a safe environment doing that thing they do without provocation throughout the night.

This side-show would occur at various times during my shift and I usually spent the rest of the evening lit off of my ass from all the free dope.

I was certain the manager was wise to my shenanigans. Or perhaps he was dumb to the fact or simply turned a blind eye. In any case, he never mentioned it. Nor did I care.

I recalled one morning, the manager - an obscenely obese, bearded queer named Bob - made a surprise visit and took over the morning shift.

Wordlessly, I stood and counted out the register. A clicking, clacking mess, beads of sweat poured down my glistening face as my teeth grinded loudly. I had been smoking dope all night and not rightly in the mood for any of his shit.

"What's the matter with you?" He inquired in that whining way fags have when asking the obvious. An aloof, bored voice laced with condescending, sneering self-importance.

Clikclikclikclik.

I straightened up, eyeballs ping-ponging around my head. Lips dry and twitching.

I sputtered, "Nothing wrong, Bob...tired. Too much coffee - just another long night chocked full of crazies, you know?"

He paused at the office entrance and stared disdainfully at my vibrating form. Eventually exhaling a dramatic sigh as only queens could who had honed the act over the years, then shuffling bitchily across the office. As he passed, waves of pungent sweat assaulted my nostrils.

Bob poured his massive buttocks into the office chair which groaned and creaked in protest, "Well, don't forget, I do have my spies here at night keeping an eye on you. So, you best be doing your job and not spending the whole shift fucking around."

I simply nodded at him with a placating smirk. I returned my attention to the register.

I hate you, you fat fuck.

All the same, as I was saying, there were the other patrons – the creepy regulars who approached the snack window vending their goodies. My sweet Dark Angels who rescued me from this horrid purgatory I duped myself into.

To win my good favor, these sallow, pale Angels - after committing acts in the theater which would have made Caligula turn away in disgust – stood in front of me all smiles, smelling of halitosis and dried semen, with fists out ready to cop a paper into my trembling paw for whatever services needed at that moment. Either in acquiring the office to smoke and/or shoot from the prying eyes of the dope pigeons or, more than often, quick sexual relief.

"Don't worry, man." They would hiss through chapped, gunk-lined lips. "I won't rat you out."

All of them were worthless, untrustworthy shits.

I thought how little the city's vice squad visited the place. Vice knowing full well the theater was a festering den of junkies and sexual perverts. The regular patrons realized this, too. All night - every night - nary a cock went unsucked or a line of speed unsorted.

One of those aforementioned regulars was my Tijuana buddy Mario who, at that moment, stood in the dank opening of the concessions window. Dark, sparkling eyes glared under black bangs.

He smirked. "Hey, white boy - howzit goin'?"

I turned and the jolt of anticipation quivered up my back. Mario was always holding.

"What's up, ya little shit? I knew you'd be here. Come on in. Make yourself comfortable."

The short Mexican swung the bottom half of the door open and entered the office. He plopped onto the overstuffed, midnight-blue lazy chair placed in front of a television which displayed the porno movies projected up onto the screen in the theater.

I grabbed a soda from a humming mini-fridge next to the cash register, and handed it to Mario, "How long you been in the theater?"

"Since 'bout one or two this afternoon." He placed the can on the dirty, tiled floor, sat up, and dug in the front pocket of his filthy jeans. He pulled out a small, plastic baggie with a zip seal to it. He held it up, black grime under the fingernails.

"I got something for ya." He said.

I grabbed the baggie and examined the white crystals inside.

Mario eyed me and grinned, "Wanna get high?"

He sing-sang it.

"You gotta ask?" I stated.

He produced from the folds of his musty clothes a small blowtorch lighter and a glass pipe - blackened and charred from use.

Retrieving a good-sized rock from the plastic bag, Mario dropped it in the end of the pipe. One end was bulbous and had a tiny opening for the dope. He placed the opposite end of the tube to his chapped lips - *flick* - and inhaled the resinous smoke into his quivering form.

Grabbing the stem from his smudged hand, I placed the tip in my mouth. While Mario held the torch, I carefully rotated the pipe left and right, watching the drug in its liquid state ooze back and forth in the bulb - greedily inhaling the grey fumes.

As soon as I passed the pipe to Mario, the shit me and hit good. A tingling jolt-like sensation culminating from the mid-back, racing up my spine to the nape of the neck, across my scalp, prickling my hairs to the forehead. A rush of Orgasmic Death.

I sank into the creaking office chair next to Mario. Our teeth ground, tongues clicking on the roofs of dry mouths. We ritualistically continued hit after hit after hit.

I shot a glance over to Mario - who sat in rapt vibrations, eyes wide and furious and intense, staring at the image of a black woman deep throating some old guy's cock flashing across the monitor.

Mario unzipped his dirty, black jeans - white and yellow verdigris crusted around the crotch - and pulled out a long, floppy, uncircumcised penis. He slid the skin back - revealing a glistening head.

"Wanna suck my cock?" He breathed; not taking his eyes off of the porn.

I stood up, placed a BACK IN 10 MINUTES sign on the concession door, and closed it. Without a word, I kneeled in front of Mario and slid my lips up and down his stiffening organ. Within minutes...*squirt!* I methodically leaned over the wastebasket...*spit!*

I returned to the office chair, Mario fumbled with his zipper, and then handed me the meth pipe. I sucked on that, too.

The acrid, metallic taste filled my lungs - my eyes darted about the office examining random objects in fleeting, yet minute, detail. Candy wrappers. Cigarette burns on the table. Pinpointing tiny debris on the floor. Time sped up and slowed down. Sped up and slowed down. The credits began rolling on the porn - I plugged another tape into the video machine. Mario popped up out of the chair.

"Okay, *cabrón*, gotta jet." His bony hand brushed his crotch, face grinning ominously, "Thanks for everything, man."

"On the contrary," I stated. "Thank you."

His face mocked concern as he glanced toward the wastebasket. "Why'd you spit it out, though? I thought you liked how I taste?"

"Can never be sure these days, right?" I answered, lighting a cigarette. I handed one to Mario. "You leavin' or gonna hang in the theater for a while?"

"I gotta meet with some stupid bitch up on 5th. I'll be back tomorrow."

"Hey, Mario," I called before he got to the exit. "Let me get a bag offa ya."

He reached into his jean jacket pocket. "I thought you might need some to get you through the night."

Mario smacked a small packet into my palm. He opened the concession door, smirking over his shoulder. "Don't do so much dope, man - that shit'll kill ya."

We both uttered *laterz* to one another as Mario cut out of the theater, and into the wet night.

I sat silently fingering the baggie in sweating fingers.

There are many ways crystal meth can be used. Swallowed by placing it into an empty gelatin capsule, mixed with water, or added to coffee. It can be chopped into a fine powder and snorted into the nose with a straw or similar utensil. You can smoke it using a glass pipe, light bulb, or aluminum foil.

For the more hardcore addicts, meth can be injected into a vein with a hypodermic syringe - the effects are faster and more intense - or mixed with water and inserted anally using a syringe without the needle, commonly recognized in the gay community as getting a *booty-bump*.

I had tried them all.

My preference? A glass pipe. The downside to that was: carry that pipe around and risk getting stopped by the cops - well, that shit could ruin your whole day. Hiding it at work from sniffing brown-nosers was too risky. There was far too much time to waste among my fellow employees and I was certain they spent more than half their shift simply sifting through random shit looking for contraband. I know I did.

So, I usually kept all my gear at home.

I closed the bottom half of the concession door which led to the theater hall. Rummaging through shelves stocked with cleaning supplies, I grabbed a roll of aluminum foil, walked back to the office chair, and sat.

I ripped off a slip of aluminum paper about seven inches long by two inches wide. On the counter, I folded the strip long ways and created a groove down the middle. I took a pinch of white, crystallized powder from the plastic bag and sprinkled the stuff carefully onto the groove. Grabbing a grimy ink pen - just the outer plastic casing - I removed the ink tube days ago, it now was a charred, warped mess - I positioned the plastic tube between my lips, and lined the far end of the straw up over the groove. Underneath the aluminum strip, I flicked my lighter and, with a steady flame, slowly heated the length of the strip.

The chemicals liquefied over the heat - evaporating into a grey, resinous smoke which I inhaled through the straw. I slowly heated the dope along the groove, patiently tilting the strip and following the grey ooze, that chemical-induced death, drawing the smoke into my charred lungs.

The euphoric effects were quick. My tongue slithered and curled in my mouth - sucking more smoke - teeth clenched, jaw chewed at nothing - sucked more smoke - the tingle spread along my body, fingers, back, forehead - the porno wavered as bitches moaned and screamed, "Fuck yeah! Oh fuck me! Yeah!"

echoing in my brain - sucked more smoke - the grey liquid slid down the groove and I followed like a champ.

I sat in the chair fidgeting, squirming - eyes ping-ponging around the small, dirty office - the florescent lights fluttered – a large cockroach skittered across dirty tiles - the rain hissed - sucked more smoke - the wall clock clicked ominously, insidiously loud - my skin felt clammy - I pinched more into the groove - *flick!whoosh!whee!* - sticky tongue licked dry lips - the taste of aluminum on the back of my throat seared - sucked more smoke.

Finally, with the dope spent, I sat there hyperventilating, twitching in spastic jerks.

My mind raced - reminiscing about a long-winded seminar during an N.A. meeting I had attended concerning the history of methamphetamine.

In a brightly lit hall, amid wafting cigarette smoke and polite coughs, I sat on an iron-folding chair surrounded by five other fiending and bored junkies. An old, pot-bellied man, who dressed like a retired cop, marched to a podium at the front of the stark room, and began his rant.

From what the old fart droned on about, amphetamine was originally synthesized in Germany in 1887 and, for several years, considered "the wonder medication in search of a disease".

Amphetamines arrived in Japan in 1919 and initially marketed as a recreational drug. That was, until its unusual side effects were discovered: irritability, aggressive behavior, anxiety, excitement, auditory hallucinations, and paranoia mixed with delusions and psychosis. (You have to admit, tweekers do tend to be pretty damn squirrely.)

Nothing was done with this new goldmine until the 1920's when experiments were conducted with the hopes that the drug could treat everything from depression to decongestion.

In the 1930s, amphetamine was marketed as Benzedrine and sold in over-the-counter inhalers to remedy nasal congestion. The decongestant became quite popular with the beat writer crowd of the late 40s – angel headed hipsters popping them Bennies for a solid kick, pops.

With the advent of World War II, the drug was used to keep the soldiers fighting. Allied

Forces used a pharmaceutical grade of amphetamine which was manufactured in chemistry labs. The Axis Forces consumed meth concocted through a process that the Nazis themselves discovered and manufactured in make-shift labs. The Japanese Kamikaze pilots used the narcotic before almost every flight because the effects caused them to be more alert and to fly for longer periods.

In Japan, after World War II, intravenous meth abuse reached epidemic proportions - since the Japanese military had large amounts of the narcotic stockpiled, made it readily available to the public. In lieu of the over-stocked surplus of the second World War, the United States used amphetamine on their military in every war since.

During the Vietnam War, American Soldiers consumed more amphetamine than the rest of the world during World War II. The United States government categorically denied this and, as usual, publicly judged the narcotic dangerous, handling the situation accordingly to habit by banning sales, and regarding it as a dangerous and illegal substance.

In spite of this, for public consumption during the 1970s and the 1980s, biker gangs such as the Hell's Angels were responsible for 90% of the methamphetamine produced in the United States.

With biker gangs, the drug earned the slang name *crank*. This was due to when the bikers needed to transport meth long distances, they would hide it in the crankcases of their motorcycles. For some time, this worked because it was virtually undetectable and the motorcycles functioned perfectly, even with the contraband hidden inside.

The monopoly the bikers held had shifted in the late 1980s with Mexican gangs/cartels manufacturing meth in Mexico and smuggling it into the U.S. The biker gangs then began purchasing it from the Mexicans because the drug was cheaper and easier than manufacturing their own.

Soon after, Mexico-based traffickers controlled the market for imported meth in the United States. While domestic meth was available, the majority seized had originated in Mexico and smuggled into the States via California, Arizona, and Texas.

Enough of the history lesson.

I'm going to explain it straight and country simple on how one gets hooked so easily: Meth is a drug which offers a unique characteristic of acting directly on the central nervous system. The drug activates certain regions of the brain to release dopamine. When dopamine is triggered, the user experiences a sudden rush of pure pleasure. Indescribable euphoria.

This being an artificially induced sensation, the high does not persist, which causes the user to crave more and more.

The brain will eventually stop the secretion of dopamine as it becomes immunized to the effect of the drug. We all realize where this leads: the user will continue consuming greater quantities, increasing the habit to an excessive level, attempting desperately to achieve that magnificent rush from the first high. That is the hook.

At the onset of my habit, I found myself doing the same – consuming more and more and more at all costs to acquire that first fantastic, orgasmic rush. A powerful euphoria the user will never again achieve. This is how the body becomes addicted to meth.

With that being said, meth also offers great aphrodisiac properties. When the addict uses the substance, it can, and does, cause the addict to develop a ravenous craving for sexual release.

Since meth is mostly used in group settings, such as nightclubs or the occasional adult theater, there certainly rises the chance the person will indulge in unsafe sexual practices. This can give rise to insidiously hazardous complications - such as an increased risk of HIV infection - among other nefarious dilemmas.

Then again, if you are a hardcore tweeker, you generally don't give a fuck anyway. I know I didn't.

My mind popped back into what I was doing.

Okay, enough, I thought.

Outside, the abysmal downpour of rain continued. Inside, the phantom moaning from the video continued. I placed the pen casing to my lips and smiled inward, as I took another hit, *Goddamn! This is some good shit!*

3

The night shift dragged on. I prepared a styrofoam cup of instant coffee. The current movie ended and, as I switched videos in the VCR, an unbearable wave of stench - one of decaying death - filled the small office space.

I glanced over to the box office window and noticed two bloodshot eyes gleaming back at me. Only the neck up was visible which revealed a bald, wrinkled head blotched with liver spots, scabs, and white flaky skin. Grey shadows encircled predatory eyes separated by a thin, hooked nose ending in long, greasy nose hairs. A toothless hole grinned which in turn caused the entire sickly face to wrinkle up.

"Uh...excuse me..." He wheezed in a high-pitched voice. His eyes - those fucking eyes with black spots in the corneas, like flawed marbles - never left my aghast gaze, no matter how I swayed and fidgeted. "Do you show any homo-erotic films at this theater?"

His voice shot up an octave at 'homo-erotic'.

"What?" I snapped, attempting my best to be snide as I could with this fucker so he would leave me alone.

Every time he exhaled; a wave of rotted matter filled the office.

"I asked if you show any homo-erotic videos in your theater." He scratched his bald head with pudgy, dirty fingers - dead, dry skin flaked off - a frayed hospital band dangled at his ashy wrist.

Under a dirty, brown overcoat, I noticed he wore a powder-blue hospital gown over a fat, squat body.

"Nah," I said, "Against city ordinance. We only show straight porn here."

His eyes glazed over as he stared at my chest.

As if in a trance, he creaked, "You see, in Manhattan - that's New York City - they screen homo-erotic videos at the cinema for grown-ups. Wonderfully, wild, exciting gay features comprised of beautiful men committing hot and passionate sex acts with one another..."

He paused, squeaking out a rapid-fire of giggles that pinged in my mind like needles. The laughter abruptly stopped.

His face went blank and dreamy, "Are there any military men in your theater?"

I pondered, took a sip of my tepid coffee, "Well, I do believe there were three navy guys who came in about an hour ago…"

Slap! Clackclack! Slam! Before I could finish my sentence, the old perv slapped six dollars down on the box office counter, bolted through the turnstile, and flew through the metal door entrance to the theater.

Five minutes passed and three, young Navy recruits stumbled out of the theater - hands over their noses, waving palms in front of their faces with looks of disgust.

"Damn! That fucker stank!"

"See how that old fag followed us everywhere?"

"Shit! His fuckin' intestines must be rotting!"

The three marched away, laughing into the night, and back to base.

A short time later, as I stood with my back to the concession door, I put the pen casing to my mouth. I casually lit up more dope from the charred strip of aluminum foil which I had stashed behind a pile of empty video boxes.

My chapped lips stung as the tube casing heated - the sharp reek of melted plastic and chemicals assailed my scarred nostrils. I stood catatonic and faced the wall. My teeth ground uncontrollably; air whistling loudly through my nose.

"Hey, man." Rumbled a baritone voice behind me.

I whirled to see a mountain of a sweaty, googly-eyed black man standing at the concession door. He wore a do-rag on his head and a torn wife-beater in a shameful attempt to cover an obscene, hairy potbelly. His face was slack; covered in a fine layer of glistening grease. He smelled of cheap bologna and stale farts.

"Yeah? Whutsup?" I wearily asked through gummy lips. My tongue swirled in my mouth like a writhing slug.

My eyes felt as if they were protruding from their sockets. I tried to keep my cool. Focusing my gaze on that glaring behemoth, I slipped the foil back behind the stack of video boxes.

"Hey, man." He repeated.

A long pause.

"Yeah? Watchawant?" I asked.

Click click click went my tongue on the clammy roof of my mouth.

"Hey." He said calmly - eyes voluminous and yellow with black irises and no color.

"What?!" I pleaded in exasperation.

The man was flying high on some wacky shit.

"You by yourself?"

"Uh..." I glanced at the baseball bat hidden next to the cash register.

He licked his thick lips with a discolored tongue.

"These movies can make ya horny."

"Glad you like the movies, sir." I croaked as I clenched my grinding jaw.

He stood a beat – ogling – his mouth had become noticeably moist.

"Hey." His eyebrows shot up and down - fat lips drooping. "Ya game? Ya wanna? Huh? Ya game? Huh? Ya game? Ya wanna?"

"Well, I can't...I mean, I'm working."

His titanic frame inert, the eyebrows continued to bounce.

"Ya wanna? Huh, boy...ya wanna? Ya game? Huh? You wanna?"

Weary of his goofy shit and desperately wanting to get back to my dope, I stated firmly, "Look, dude, you gotta stop bugging me. Return to the theater or I'm gonna hafta ask you to leave."

He remained inert, glaring with that vapid gaze of Hepatitis C and panting noticeably loud through flared nostrils. Then, without another word, faded back into the murk of the cinema.

4

I sat in the foul-smelling recliner adjacent two television monitors. One displayed an Asian cooch who slobbered on the half-hard cocks of three grinning college studs lounging on a red couch. The other monitor was the image of the security camera which rendered a static, black and white view of the sidewalk outside the box office window and entrance to the theater.

Like clockwork, an elderly, white-haired relic in lime green pants, yellow polo shirt, and white baseball cap stood for hours night after night. His rattling dentures chewed obsessively on a wad of gum in a mouth that was a glistening, wet hole. Squinted, rheumy eyes darted up and down the sidewalk. His torso never moved. He remained poised in a gung-ho position as if he was prepared to pounce on whatever victim he deemed worthy. From his pant pocket, the only movement was a right hand which jiggled his loose change.

Chink, chink, chink.

A tall, rotund man in khaki shorts and summer shirt darted past the elderly perv and quickly strolled up to the box office window.

He pressed his bearded face against the pane which caused condensation from his hot breath to form on the glass.

"Hey, dude." He rumbled in a distinct southern Californian accent. "I don't wanna see a movie. I just wanna buy some porn."

My boss sold a vast library of accumulated pornography that he hoarded in the office. Occasionally, some creepy connoisseur of filth would come in off the street, or from the theater, and purchase one or two videos for their collection.

I stood up, walked to the window, and buzzed the man in from a button next to the register, "Okay, come on in."

I flopped back into the easy chair.

Behind the recliner, taking up the entire wall on a black-lacquer bookshelf, were six tiers of porn. All types of nasty shit. From straight-laced, crack-addicted blonde bitches to those gay fisting horrors. Scores of glossy boxes were covered in dust and smudged fingerprints. The bottom shelf held candies, dried ramen soups, and small bags of pre-popped popcorn.

The man appeared at the concessions window, "May I come in?"

"Yeah, sure," I said.

I didn't look at him; my gaze was focused on the flickering images of bouncing flesh on the monitor. My high was cranking down and I wanted to get that fat fucker out quick.

"Lessee lessee lessee..." He breathed as he perused the selection. He would occasionally pick up a box, scan the back, and replace it with a "Hmmm. Oh. Hmmmm..."

Ding! Someone was at the box office. I rose from my seat to see an emaciated meth junkie who stood outside. A myriad of small reddish-brown scabs stood out from ghastly pale skin. The eyes were sunken in a withered skull, the stubbled jaw chewed loudly.

"How much, man? How much ta git up in this bitch?" He spastically spat.

"Six dollars. You can stay until six in the morning when I shut down for an hour and clean up." I droned.

His head darted from side to side, "Right. Gimme a ticket."

He slapped the bills on the counter. I handed him his ticket and buzzed him in. I returned to the easy chair and flopped back down.

The fat bastard who was perusing the porn - the fucking pervert – stood in front *over* me, brazenly swaying his bloated, hairy belly in my face. He smelled of cheap lotion and sweat. I outwardly grimaced as I noticed a small lump moving within his cargo shorts. Asshole thought I must be an easy score.

Fuck that, I got standards!

I waved my hand in front of his pasty gut, "Hey, man, cut that fucking shit out! You wanna buy a video or what?"

The fat slob took a step back.

As if nothing had transpired, he continued to casually scan the selection of tapes, "Nah...nothing here that interests me. Just gimme a ticket for the theater."

He reached into the pocket of his cargo shorts. His hand adjusted his small, throbbing organ. He then whipped out a folded stack of single bills; counted six dollars.

I bolted up exasperated, snatching the bills from his semen-stained hand, and passed him a red ticket at arm's length. Nonchalantly, he walked through the dingy, velvet curtains into the cinema.

"Asshole," I hissed under my breath.

I shook my head in disgust as a middle-aged black man abruptly popped up in front of the concession stand.

"Hey, boy! Got you workin' all night, again?" He smiled broadly, which was an appalling thing to witness.

His eyes bulged out of their sockets; the large skull could hardly contain the distorted, charcoal-colored skin which stretched over it. Deeply grooved like that of a corpse, the voluminous lips were white and chapped. I found his face somewhat comical. A bewildered visage of no more than prominent eyes and lips.

Being a regular customer, I had seen this cat before. He usually arrived before my shift and remained all night doing his dope. He never caused any problems and kept to himself.

"Hey, man, how's the theater?" I smiled back as I placed the money from the previous pervert into the register.

"Sheeeet! It gettin' crazy in there." He rolled egg-sized eyes in sallow sockets. "It looks like a damn rock concert with them lighters flickin' all ovuh." We both chuckled as he continued, "You hungry?"

Before I could answer, the box office doorbell rang, and on the monitor, I noticed a pizza delivery boy.

I glanced at the screen and then back to the junkie at the concession widow, "You ordered pizza?"

"Yeah! It here?" He slobbered. "You want some?"

"Hell, yeah," I said.

I buzzed the delivery guy in and the junkie paid. I grabbed a folding chair from the office and sat with the junkie at the entrance to the main cinema.

Between the steel door which led out of the building and the cinema, there lay a short, dark hallway connecting the concession window and the entrance to the theater itself. The door to the cinema was draped in a set of mildew spotted, rose-colored velvet curtains.

The junkie plopped down on an extra folding chair by the entrance.

To this day, and I cannot fathom why, various patrons chose to sit or stand at the draped entrance, hence the extra folding chair. I presumed the back seating gave them privacy from being seen by the audience while they beat their meat, or allowed them to cruise potential victims who already sat in the theater, or perhaps it was simply to mask guilt of association. A mystery that will fade into the shadows of time unanswered.

We placed the pizza box on the dirty, carpeted floor and began chomping. He then pulled a small, glass pipe from his shirt pocket, positioning it up to his lips - *flick!* As he inhaled the smoke, the cherry made a muted, crackling sound.

I smiled at him, cocking my head inquisitively, "Hey, what's that? Speed?"

The junkie exhaled, "Nah, white boy, dis here crack. Ever do it?"

"Nope," I replied.

"You wanna?" He asked.

"Sure. Why not?" I uttered.

I took the charred, glass stem from his gnarled and ashy hands. I placed the end to my lips as he ignited his lighter. Popping sounds emitted from the crack as I sucked in the grey smoke.

"Hold it in...hold it in." He coaxed.

Master and student.

The general effect was similar to meth. However, the rush was quicker and far more intense. My heartbeat tripled and my breath shortened. I could feel the blood pumping into my face. I trembled uncontrollably as if wrapped in a freakish orgasm. The euphoria one gets from crack is indescribable.

He leaned close, took the pipe from my limp hand, smirked. "Now don't go and hava heart attack, boy."

I sat and felt the drug chaotically bounce around in my system. A rush of pleasant heat flushed through my body as I clicked and twitched in jerking movements.

On the large screen in front of me, a black stud slid in and out of a blonde bimbo with rapid ferocity. She screamed and squealed in amped-up, cocaine-induced passion. Her face contorted, her eyes bugged, and gleamed in smeared eyeliner. Her locks cascaded across a seemingly terrified face with each vicious, rapid-fire thrust. A body wet with sweat; the black stud pumped with the intense concentration of a maniacal killer frozen on a scowling face.

All colors and smells in the theater were crisp and perceptible. Florescent strobes from the movie were distinctly alienated from the various aromas of chlorine, sour feet, farts, and dried semen. I felt ecstatic, euphoric, *superhuman* - a chaotic, warm glow enveloped me as nostalgic images raced through my electrocuting mind.

Then, the feeling rapidly ebbed away until only a sad, longing remained.

What the fuck? I thought. *What happened?*

Face forward, eyes sweeping in his direction, I asked, "It supposed to switch off like that?"

"Yup." He passed over the pipe, "That's why you take another hit, white boy."

I did. As the junkie devoured his pizza like a veracious chipmunk, I sucked on that glass pipe so nasty.

Once again the hot, pinging buzz enveloped me on a cellular level. I sat and took it all in, tapping both feet on the floor as if running in place while the drug took hold. Then, a few short minutes later, it sputtered out like an old generator.

"Goddamit!" I muttered.

I began to put the pipe back to my mouth.

The junkie stopped me with a foul-smelling hand, "Hey, hey, boy - this shit ain't free. You want some more, slip me a fiddy. I'll give ya and yer good to go."

Fuck that shit! Fifty dollars for a rock? That gave me - what? Two, three hits? Shit, for fifty dollars I could get five or six good, fat lines of meth and be 'good to go' for eight hours or more straight.

I stood up and wiped the grease from the pizza off of my hands onto my jeans.

"I gotta get back to work," I mumbled.

"You gonna leave me like dat? You ain't gonna buy no shit o' wut?"

"Nah," I mumbled with my back to him, folding the metal chair. "Uh, thanks. I'll be in the office."

"Ain't dat some shit." He retorted.

I returned to the office and reached behind the pile of porn boxes for my aluminum strip. As I took a hit off of the residue, I glanced at the security monitor. There stood the old, white man. *Chink chink chink.*

5

The hissing of the rain continued as I glanced out the box office window. Yellow streetlamps lit a blue, plastic tarp covering the upper part of a bulky form. Like a walking pile of dirty rags glistening in the half-dark, a stooped, homeless man soggily pushed a shopping cart overburdened with his dreams down the wet, grey sidewalk.

I grabbed my notebook and jotted down notes. I seemed to be following a fractured nightmare. The high which wracked my body was winding down and I began to feel depressed. More than usual.

I stared at my dog-eared copy of a book by Charles Bukowski which lay on the counter next to me and I sighed. The more I read his work, and the works of Kerouac, Burroughs, Orwell, Hemingway, Selby - the more distasteful my writing style appeared to me. I recognized those novelists as my superiors.

They could take a few choice words and produce beautiful flowers.

I saw myself as a writer writing unpublishable horrors. I inwardly frowned, realizing full well that I would be living in shit and degradation until my dying day – eventually found slumped in a chair, face ashen grey with age as I clutched my final work. How maudlin.

Thirty years later, students would be scrutinizing and analyzing my works at Harvard and Yale with a pigeon dung-covered bronze statue of my ravaged ass erected outside the literary building. Life was funny that way, I reckoned.

A kaleidoscope of images flashed across my fucked up mind. I didn't scribble in my tiny, uniformed, capital letters of sensational tales concerning blonde heroes careening across the solar system battling intelligent octopi or warrior insects. I began to write about my loneliness. Focusing on how I continued to obsess over the wreck of a past four-year relationship. O! How the world was brighter and far more comprehensive back then. I sat in a funk and meditated on the life-shattering pain of that separation.

I recalled the day after he and I had separated: Back in Los Angeles, the sun was glaringly bright; green palm trees slowly rustled from a gentle wind. In a swanky bar on Santa Monica Boulevard, I stood beat and forlorn accompanied by a simpering, short fag in tight black clothes and dangling, bleached locks. He leaned next to me – striking that pose fags do when striving to look nonchalant in any establishment; arms and feet crossed, limply holding a watered-down drink.

The bar was not that crowded - *Rage* it was called. Homosexual clones posed around us in their uniform of white tank tops, jeans, and black work boots.

On every face, they fearlessly brandished phantom masks of sadness and lost desperation with that subtle gleam of scorning hatred no amount of alcohol consumed could hide. The common gay attitude face.

My diminutive colleague, who I had known for some time, glanced at me earnestly, "So, whacha gonna do now? I realize how much breaking up with him must pain you."

Pain me? Oh, the overdramatic pain I felt raging inside as I stood in Rage surrounded by a gaggle of raging queens who I wanted nothing more than see incinerated in a blast of atomic destruction. The pain! It felt so insidious! Like a corkscrew jabbed in the heart. During the previous four years, I had a reason to get up in the morning, to shower, eat, work, to live, and love, with all those sweet, candy-colored memories and emotions that danced along with it. Now, there was a hole - a deep, sorrowful, dark void in my chest so fucking ugly to feel and sense and smell.

I took a sip of my rum and coke and sighed, "I'm going to take a weekend vacation. To Tijuana, I guess. Cool off, you know? Think things over."

"Tijuana?!" The elfish fag shrilled. "Mexico? Why there?"

Internally, I wanted to die. What else was there to live for? Anyone who has had their heart broken and was prone to overdramatic responses to certain situations would understand my motives.

I concluded, at the time, there was no reason for me to go on. I thought of suicide on several occasions - the drudge of jumping through life's rut with all its hate and anger and paranoia and never-ending letdowns - all seemed pointless. It felt fruitless to continue to placate the two-faced condescending queers of West Hollywood or perhaps it was simply the mortification of gazing into my colleague's eyes and realizing full well they were laughing internally, "Haha! You got dumped!"

On a spiritual level, I believed suicide was not an option. Personally, and I wouldn't have it any other way, if God was up there, I truly believed (or at least thought) He forgave all things, save the act of suicide. At least that was what I remembered from Sunday school. Why exchange one Hell for another? That belief stayed my hand during several attempts.

I realized I needed to attempt the sinister act precariously. Vicariously. I chose to venture into the most dangerous city I knew and that was Tijuana, Mexico. I visited the city only twice prior in my life and knew next to nothing of the locale; save the whispered horror stories from beaten and long-winded acquaintances who journeyed there on occasion.

I embraced the half-hoped fantasy I would go down there, wave fistfuls of dollars around in several dismal bars, and at the crack of a foggy dawn, the police would find me face down in a shit-strewn alley with no pants - my life pumped out of me. Thus ending the gnawing hurt in my heart over that angst-ridden separation.

Unlike Lot's wife, I didn't look back. I packed the few clothes which would fit in my small duffel bag and purchased a cheap Mexican bus line to the Tijuana border. I lived in a crappy room above a whorehouse for the first six months undertaking ghastly things.

That long-ago weekend of supposedly self-reflection stretched into years of insidious suffering. The guilt, the depression, and pain which I felt, enveloped my soul and consumed my world.

Once settled in Tijuana, I soon became acquainted with Plaza Santa Cecilia. The Plaza was the central nervous system of gay Tijuana. A stretch of pedestrian concrete which spanned diagonally from Revolution to Constitution Avenue and Second Street, topped off by a silver slash across the sky, the Millennium Arch.

Scattered throughout the Plaza were sidewalk cafes offering open tables 24/7 where old, American queers sat entertaining up to four or five boys at a time.

Those decaying fags giggled and shrieked and rolled their eyes at one another in vain attempts to impress their American colleagues at how popular they could still be with younger men. The cruising fags lounged in the shade of the arched columns of the café as they would coo and screech, flipping wrists and rolling eyes, tearing one another apart with catty, gay double-entendre. The hustlers loitered and smiled and laughed at the right times, waiting to rob those festering, old vampires of every peso they owned.

The male prostitutes of Plaza Santa Cecilia fit in a unique classification. I had never before perceived their equal for importunity and all-around obnoxiousness. They were, without fail, attracted to the uncoordinated movements of the American in a strange land. The least show of not knowing precisely where you were going and they would run at you from their lurking places in the sidebars and cafés.

"Want nice chico, meester?"

"See bullfight? Donkey Show?"

"Want mota?"

"Nice boy? Show you good time?"

"You like beeg one, meester?"

There was a never-ending procession of hustlers of all types to choose from. All patrolling the Plaza with the attitude of aroused Tomcats.

In the middle of Plaza was the notorious cantina *Bar Ranchero* - one of several gay locales which ringed the square. It was renowned for its unconcealed seediness. A hotbed of blatant, cruising homosexuals, rough hustlers, American pedophiles, and drug addicts.

The interior of the bar was a low-ceiling room. On one side stretched a long counter tended by two, tough lesbians. The cantina held a small dance floor which catered to strippers and tired drag shows; and one could dance on it if one felt inclined.

On the other side of the bar lined old, rickety, metal chairs and tables where sex and drugs were bought with indifference. Against the back wall, a jukebox played the same tunes over and over again. Next to that was the entrance to the mensroom - a virtual carnival in which drugs flowed as easily as the piss. Oral sex was openly common. I had witnessed acts that would have caused Caligula to blush.

And, in the middle of the cantina on the main floor, rentboys and queens stood and posed, gazing out with probing, calculating lust.

I soon became a fixture of this dive and developed friendships with many of the hustlers who frequented the cantina. They were hopped up on meth so as to remain awake 24/7 and woo their various clients. It was through these diabolical cocksuckers I received my first major taste of speed.

I was partying and living in such liberation, one unlike I'd ever encountered in Los Angeles. However, I still bore a black cloud over my head and began consuming more and more methamphetamines. It seemed to alleviate the pain I harbored from that romantic wreck.

The once in a while sniffs in cantina toilet stalls eventually led to a full blown addiction.

I learned the meaning of absolute need.

All I desired was my writing and my dope. I kept a detailed journal and transcribed my experiences living in the whore district with painful accuracy. I never meant to publish any of the tripe - I always considered it *a letter*. A letter of desperate woe to send to the ex-lover who destroyed my heart. I wanted him to feel the desperation and heartache in that I fostered. And yet, as time passed, and with all things - I simply did not care anymore. About him. About my previous life in Los Angeles. Nothing mattered. Nothing but my writing and my meth.

Life is funny like that. One day, you are drudging through the worst emotional trauma of your life, and a week later, who gives a shit, right?

But, that was then...

In the office of the theatre, I sat the notebook down. In scribbling handwriting, the words *See what you did? See what you put me through? I am living this toxic, bitter, sad existence and it is entirely YOUR fault! I hate you! I hate you so fucking much for doing this to me!* banefully stood out in black against the white paper. Waves of depression washed over my shriveled torso. I picked up the crinkly, aluminum strip. Nothing. The little plastic baggie licked dry. I sighed and walked toward the concession window, hanging the BACK IN TEN MINUTES sign on the door as I closed it.

I decided to confront my frump with a little release.

In the darkened theater, the air was thick with sweat, dried semen, and the grunts and moans of uninhibited lust.

On-screen, an Asian cooch was getting banged in the back seat of a convertible as they drove down the freeway. Porno was scratching the bottom of the barrel if it had to succumb to such cheap thrills.

Speaking of cheap thrills, I sat in the back row when a short Mexican, who slouched one seat down from me, whipped out a glass pipe and, with a small blow torch, began smoking crack without reservations.

I sat and listened to the crackle and pop of the drug mixed with the shrieking of the she-bitch onscreen, I smelled the aroma of said crack and the tingle of tired, old cells began to activate.

The little Mexican - I had seen him several times before - sat with his unattractive, frog-like face shimmering in a fine layer of perspiration.

He handed over the pipe, "Hey, man, want some?"

Ugh, don't wanna have sex with you.

"Nah." I croaked. "I don't do that shit anymore."

"Don't do it anymore?" He asked mechanically. "What do you do now?"

"I write. (*cough*) I'm a writer."

"Really?" He took another obscene drag. "What do you write?"

I started glassy eyed into the dark and said solemnly, "Garbage."

Ah, fuck it, I thought.

I looked towards him, reaching, "May I?"

"Sure, man...it's only dope."

Click - fffft - wheeeeeee!

Small, white sparks exploded behind my eyes as my body felt that 240-watt current.

"Damn." I quivered.

"Yup." The Mexican smacked his thick lips. "Surefire way to wipe away them blues."

After a few more hits, I was a clicking, teeth-grinding, jittery mess. The Mexican poofed away in an incandescent mist.

Shrouded in tattered clothes, a Fagin-looking hobo character entered and plopped next to me, reeking like last week's sewage.

"Hey, buddy." He wheezed halitosis into my face. "You wanna get high?"

In the murk, his eyes glistened, resembling a nocturnal predator. His oily, razor-thin face glared at me with obvious lust.

"No." I sneered. "Drugs are for losers."

"Suit yer fuckin' self." He hissed.

Fagin vibrated out of focus a shivering, teeth-grinding wreck. I was left alone with some little Yoda-looking coot ogling and grinning, jiggling change in his pocket.

Side note: In all my years as a homo in the service, why was it in these porno joints there was always, and I mean *always*, some fucking Elder who would stand for hours on end smacking gum or jiggling change in their polyester pant pockets? Annoying old fucks.

Time to move on. Whacked it a few as the movie heated up and the older queens did their dance of seduction around me. I ignored the lot of them. They were not worthy.

That was until a clean-cut, college-type jock sprung up from the front rows. I noticed he was sniffing and bounced around the theater like a ping-pong ball. He walked back to the hall leading to the toilet. Old perverts raised their heads like animals sensing danger. New Meat. The Exodus to the mensroom ensued; leaving me alone.

I repaired to the loo to wash off my hands - old, bitter fairies paraded in a stylized ballet of random, broken lust amid sounds of pissing and farting. The smell of bleach, semen, and shit lingered in the foul, graffitied room.

Sitting back in the theater proper, I glanced around and the late-night fun fest was in full swing. Heads bobbed in crotches of willing patrons as the desperate and depraved prowled through the aisles.

An attractive hipster kid who I had noticed before, slithered next to me and performed the most mind-blowing blow job on me I have had in many a moon. Afterward the bitch slunk away and gave a repeat performance on a muscular black man before I even had the chance to say thank you.

My immediate vicinity was a London fog of grey carcinogens. I sat silently puffing on a cigarette in a row of crackheads and observed the show around me; not paying much attention to the tasteless vulgarity performed on the screen.

My shift was nearly over, it was time to close up and clean the filthy joint out. I returned to the office and counted out the register. Tallying the stock and marking down the inventory in the ledger books.

At the stroke of 6 am, I switched the video off and flicked on the main lights. The sounds of anguished grunts and sighs of desperation rose from the theater's patrons.

I grabbed the microphone connected to the speaker system and droned in the most faux professional voice I could muster, "Attention, theater goers! It is 6am and the theater is now closed. If you wish to return...please come back at 7:30 after the theater has been cleaned. Tickets can be bought either at the concession window or at the box office. Thank you."

The speakers whined silent.

The exodus of perverts and junkies streamed out of the cinema. I stood at the box office window and with a placating grin on my face, watched as they shuffled out.

Stopping at the window, swaggered old Carl. An African American who dressed in funky, 1970s pimp clothes – multi-patterned silk shirt, flared slacks, white, patent-leather shoes, and a snap brimmed mesh hat. His face was a ravaged map of creases and scars with dust and grease in the cracks. His eyes squinted and voluminous lips held an irreversible grimace.

He situated himself outside of the box office window, and drawled, "Look, my man, gimme one of dem tickets fo' 7:30 and I'll hook you up wit some fine ass shit."

"Yeah?" I asked. "Whacha got, Carl?"

His eyes rolled around in his skull as he slid an ashy hand across crusted, dry lips, "Mmmm, yeah. I got dis shit fo ya, white boy. Good shit."

He pulled a small, pink baggie from the folds of his shirt.

I took it and handed him a ticket, "Thanks, Carl."

I curiously glanced at the pink/white powder in the bag.

He examined the ticket, "Wit dis I can come back in, right? No problems?"

"Yep. Just give that ticket to the dude who relieves me."

He turned toward the street, stopped, and snapped his fingers in thought, "Right - right. Now, listen up, that some strong shit. Don't do it all at once, 'k?"

I shrugged with my hands open and smiled, "C'mon, I'm a big boy, Carl."

"Shiiiiiit...." He chuckled in laughter which sounded like an unoiled machine and walked out into the predawn mist.

It seemed almost every night was the same, after shooing everyone out, there always was some reeking flop snuggled into a chair snoring, and no manner of poking, screaming, or dousing with water was going to stir him. The trick was to simply hoist him up and drag him out. Usually, he awakened, kicking and screaming, and that's when you had to get tough with the fucker.

This morning was no different as I held the door open and violently pushed the old bum out - *whack!* - he bounced off the door frame, and with another push, went rolling into the street cursing; face red with rage.

I locked up the office and headed toward the storage closet. I grabbed the mop and bucket. I stood a moment, gazing at the lit theater with its rows of stained chairs and wooden floor carpeted with cigarette butts.

I am going to explain it to you and I'm going to explain it to you country simple: There is nothing more grotesque and demeaning than cleaning a porno theater after 24 hours of use by a legion of cum guzzling perverts and filthy junkies.

Donning industrial-rubber gloves and broom in hand, I went to work. Sweeping

73

between the isles, I found used condoms, wadded tissue, watches, underclothes, glass pipes, syringes, and dope. And always money. On a good night, I could score up to one hundred dollars in loose bills. Drunks were always spilling money from their pockets in fumbling fits of passion.

I slopped water into a hideous bucket and mopped away all the coating of saliva, mucus, and semen.

Onto the mensroom; which had blossomed into a biological horror. I used bleach abundantly, searing my eyes and nostrils, taking time to spray down the sink, urinal, and toilet with an entire can of Lysol – thickly coating down the glory hole in the graffitied scrawled toilet wall.

I know you're all like *ew*, but more often than not, I usually employed one of the regular crackheads who would clean just to remain indoors, not having the extra six dollars for readmission. These junkies would jump at the chance because of the money and dope they knew they'd find lying around under the seats.

However, that morning I was feeling it. In a tweeking fit of dope-induced energy, I scrubbed that theater spotless. I did leave one corner seat caked in dried, chunky vomit and urine. I have my limits.

After I vacuumed the carpet in the halls, I returned to the office to reopen the theater and waited for my shift to end.

An hour passed and my relief arrived, a scrawny white kid with a scraggly, black goatee named David. He was a tattooed musician in a floundering garage band and a student who attended writing classes at the Community College. He was also ass deep in heroin addiction.

I recalled a few weeks prior as I sat in the office, one of Bob's slimy, beetle-looking friends appeared at the concession window not only to buy a candy bar but also to vomit out gossip he had accumulated on David. Gossip, I was certain, that caused the creepy little fucker gastronomic problems holding in all day.

The short, rotund pervert confided in hushed tones when he came to the concession window earlier during David's shift, the young man was slumped on the nod in the office chair, hunched over, with tongue hanging out, right hand clutching a syringe.

I was convinced Bob had heard about the incident. But, since David was handsome in that Calvin Kline junky model way, the fat fuck turned a blind eye.

David was not bad as far as people went, timid, reserved - hopelessly heterosexual - and every morning I met him, he loved to relate the horror stories of his previous day's work shift.

"You know that old man with the bag? The red canvas shopping bag?" David began as soon as he entered the office.

"Yeah? The one who looks like Uncle Fester?" I asked, mixing a cup of instant coffee.

The man in question was a regular who would frequent the porno theater every day (There are different varieties of addiction, I suppose. Drugs. Alcohol. Porn. Food. Being a little bitch.) and I was positive the man was one of Bob's squealers.

"Yup, that's him," David said as he placed his book bag on the blue recliner. "People were saying he would troll around the theater - y'know, looking for dick - and when someone would refuse his advances, he would stand up dramatically, turn, and fart on them as he walked away."

I smirked because I'd seen it happen.

David tore a sheet of paper towel off a roll and taped it across the monitor showing the porn on the theater screen.

I looked over at him as he adjusted the sheet of paper and stated, "Heh, you always do that."

He stood up, hands on hips, examining the monitor to make certain no filth filtered through, "That shit can rot your brains and can cause impotency, man!"

I inwardly shrugged. Who am I to judge?

I passed off any pertinent information, said my goodbyes, and walked out into the shimmering dawn.

The streets were still wet from the previous night's downpour. However, the sky was a brilliant blue as an orange sun came screaming over the horizon. The sidewalks were empty as I trudged up to a station to jump a trolley back to the border.

As I stood and waited at the stop, a young transvestite adorned in a black dress, bright blue wig, black horn-rimmed glasses, red garter belt outside the dress, and old-style, high-top sneakers, silently peddled past on a beach cruiser bicycle in the still dawn. As she whisked by, I nonchalantly hummed the Witch's theme from *The Wizard of Oz*.

The train ride back to the border was a painful ordeal. Everything seemed to be in sharp focus and amplified. A group of American tourists were being exceptionally loud and all I thought about was killing them. One by one. Violently and over-dramatically. I digress, I am not a psychopath.

I desired a beer. I hopped the border and made my way through those teeming Mexican masses - brown, bloodshot eyes followed my every move - to the Plaza and entered *Bar Ranchero*.

During that time of the morning, the joint was empty, save for a small knot of screeching, gesticulating fags and two hung-over drag queens at one end of the bar.

In a corner chair, a fat, crimson-faced American tourist sat passed out, leaning against the wall. The pockets of his cargo shorts turned inside out – his shoes missing; revealing dirty socks.

I stomped over to the counter and ordered a drink. Taking a table, it was only a matter of seconds before I was accosted by the local 'buy me a beer, meester' boys.

"Beat it! I didn't move down here to support your worthless asses!" I spat.

One of the three seemed mortally wounded.

Mario entered the cantina and sat with me. We sat for a full five minutes without saying a word. Obviously, we both were recovering from a long night.

I finally croaked, "You holdin'?"

Under the table, he slipped me a paper and I handed him 100 pesos. I walked into the bathroom - a white-tiled den of penis peepers, cock suckers, and pervs.

I found an empty stall and closed the door.

In the stall next to me, I heard the telltale sign of sniffing, and on the adjacent side, the slurping of an anonymous rentboy earning a cheap room to sleep. The smell of shit, piss, and chlorine wafted in the moist air.

I emptied my package onto the toilet paper dispenser and chopped out three lines with an old credit card - thanking God it now had a purpose. Rolled up a 20 peso note into a cylinder and *snort-wheeee! snort-whoop!*

Slowly, I stood straight up, my fucked-up gaze focusing on obscene graffiti on the tile wall, and asked myself, *Why? Why do I continue to do this to myself?*

Any addict will confess that it is a well-known fact - a tired, long-winded, overstated fact - that addiction comes from the course of pain and misery. And, I had that in spades.

No use pining over it now, I thought. *I can quit whenever I want.*

Scratched my nose with my forefinger, I checked for residue.

Returning to my table, I found Mario had gone, and I finished three, quick beers.

I struck up a conversation with an attractive, bespectacled lad named Javier and he being quite literary. Well read. We sat and chatted over authors - Kerouac, Selby, Bukowski, Vonnegut, Kafka, Genet. He was familiar with all my favorites.

Around 11am, we found ourselves in a hotel and doing that which nature doesn't abide. We fucked and sucked and licked and poked. Yet, I felt nothing. I merely went through the motions.

As Javier lay asleep, his right arm and leg wrapped around me - my mind spun. I smoked a cigarette and stared at the yellow splotches on the ceiling. I thought of the new book I had begun. This one began at my birth and related to the story of my adolescence. The brutal, despondent parents, the sad school days, the ravaged coming of age. I thought the title fit: *Fried Chitlins*. Grey and disgusting. That put me into an even more frump.

I lay thinking thinking thinking - smoking smoking smoking.

Perhaps I needed a bit of road traveling. A little adventure through Mexico. Something. I held no goal or plan for my life and that seriously concerned me. My life was so open, so free - yet, so fitfully alone. I seemed as if I couldn't connect with the human species. I felt apart. Adrift. On a poisoned river with no end in sight.

When Javier drowsily rolled over, I slowly rose, silently dressed, and left the room.

The sun swung high overhead. I found a hotdog vendor on Revolucion Avenue and stood there munching; watching the hung-over tourists drag themselves back to the border, watching patrol cars creep by, the transvestite hookers clomp around.

I stood under that dazzling midday sky and thought, *There has to be more to this life. Is this all there is? This is life, dumbass.*

I hailed a taxi and went home.

Home. The apartment was near the end of a blind alley which hardly received any sun. I slid the key into the metal door and stepped into the dank.

The air was stagnant and particles danced in the beams of yellow sunlight through drawn curtains. The two-room apartment was small and grimy. Movie posters of underground directors such as David Lynch and John Waters cluttered the walls and dirty laundry and empty fast-food wrappers littered a soiled, red carpet.

The bedroom itself contained a well-worn queen-sized bed with a black oak headboard, and matching nightstand.

The living room was occupied by a black futon, a small table, and a window that looked out into a filthy, garbage-littered alley. A dusty ceiling fan wobbled above.

The bathroom contained wall-to-wall-to-floor white tiles, a porcelain sink, and a toilet. The old kind which had a latch and a chain you pulled from above. There was a mildew-covered shower which had a tap that reluctantly squirted tepid water.

The kitchen was comprised of an old, dented, mint-colored refrigerator from the '50s that still ran, a sink area, a stove, and a metal table with two metal chairs. All furnishings could be considered antiques.

Not a bad place, near Zona Rosa, and close enough to the border so I could walk or if in need of a hasty exit.

Still feeling the methamphetamine, I sat in my room with my notebook and scribbled out a few more anecdotes in my new book. I held nothing back - inscribing raw, peeled tales of a horrible, sorrowful past.

After a few hours, as I sat in the dim room smoking my umpteenth cigarette, I concluded I had indeed found my calling. But, to what end?

6

All the broken streets of the city led downward between deepening chasms of masonry to a vast, rectangular-shaped Plaza full of shadows. Faded, candy-colored adobe walls of *la placita* were perforated by dwelling cubicles and cafes, some a few feet deep, others extended out of sight into a network of dank rooms and graffitied corridors obscured by rank mist and steam. Belching from the myriad warrens, overpowering smells of stale *frijoles*, seared meat, mota, and shit assaulted the senses. With brazen arrogance, drunken Americans stumbled through the plaza as they, in turn, were manhandled by transsexual deviants of all categories. Beckoning with flashes of silver teeth, catatonic, emaciated whores stood grey and withered in the doorless entrances of their diseased cubicles of Viral Death.

Nevertheless, there was tequila-induced vomiting in the streets as salsa music blared and truckloads of police rumbled through. The dusty paddy wagons kicked up grit as the baneful screams of the day's prey wailed in anguish from the windowless, steel canopies attached to the rear of each vehicle. Spattered angel wings covered with soot, their moans reverberated under a neon heaven – angels in Hell they, their broken wings huge in the dark.

Entering an apartment building dark and sinister, I made my way down fetid feces smelling hallways with green walls flaking like sclerosis. I came into a patio in the middle of the building with an opening to a cloudless sky.

Then I saw eight, maybe ten other people who milled about the corners with charred glass pipes and flicking lighters – all of them junkies. Rugged and suffering features covered terminally sick faces of beaded sweat. Eyes alert, mouth alert – all worked swiftly on pipe hits. Orange flames sparked in the smokey gloom. Everyone was lighting up.

I smoked my fill and faded out, back into the crowded streets.

An old man draped in colorless, filthy rags blinked in the unrelenting Mexican sun. His face creased with the hue of a brown paper bag and he sported a dingy, yellow cowboy hat. He watched out of tired and rheumy eyes as three white Ford trucks - *Tijuana paddy wagons* - hurtled down a broad street, kicking up dust. The dust stung his eyes, yet he stood immobile. Several police officers clung to the sides as they raced by - dark eyes filled with fear, hatred - their caramel-colored faces hidden in black ski masks.

One stared back at the old man, fingering his shiny, black AK-47. The old man stood stooped glaring in sadness. Seconds later and blocks away, gunfire and rumbling explosions. As the street teemed with pedestrians casually going about their affairs, five more trucks hurtled passed, followed by monstrous paramilitary vehicles.

I stood in the coolness of an awning, sucking on a cigarette with the vibrant backdrop greenery of Park Teniente Guerrero behind me. It was hot. Humid. My shirt clung to my person like a used condom. Three squad cars roared by as sirens howled, startling an Indian mother clutching a frail baby to her breast. Five dirty children raced behind her, skillfully crossing the street congested with kamikaze taxis and rickety buses belching black smoke. Several *milandros* turned and hid their faces from the barreling convoy. Ever since the local cartel executed 46 of them the week prior, the municipal police always traveled by car in threes. Their faces cold and featureless masks of fear and suspicion.

I somewhat recalled two nights prior in my room, hearing the *ratatatat* of machine gunfire in the distance, I quickly flung myself onto the dusty tiled floor strictly from habit. Last night the symphony repeated itself down on the corner. Seven bodies lay akimbo in the darkened lamppost splashed street; blood oozed onto black concrete and *vecinos* didn't care. Thirty minutes later, a fat cop chewed a cigar stump surveying the scene.

In the rural hills of *colonia Independencia* where you can score for mota, speed, heroin, coke, crack - anything your junky heart desired - fires ran rampant in the shanty-like adobes.

Outside the high, white-washed walls of a crumbling school, a five-year-old boy timidly scuttled home clutching his textbooks past roving gangs of cholos, their tattooed faces vicious in hate, openly brandishing pistols to deter the inquiring *placas.*

Yet, down on Avenida Revolucion, the arrogant tourist still reveled, still drank, still danced, still bought that *One-tequila, two-tequila, three-tequila...floor!* t-shirt that they just must have for the folks back home in Wisconsin, unaware of the slaughter occurring a few blocks from their reverie. This was Tijuana - *my Tijuana* - a place I called home.

7

Unlike common people who work graveyard shift, I never directly went to sleep on account of being hopped up on so much speed by the time I arrived home. That morning was no exception.

I undressed and lay on my bed completely naked. For a few minutes I remained immobile, my raw eyes transfixed on the orange stains which splotched the ceiling paint from a leaky roof.

I grabbed the baggie of meth from my shirt pocket I had received from Carl earlier. I held it up to my face and meticulously scrutinized it. The color was off. It had flecks of blue embedded in the usual whiteness of the dope.

"Don't do it all," I whispered his warning.

I snatched my glass pipe from the end table and carefully held it in my thumb and forefinger. Momentarily pondering that such a small thing was capable of providing so much insidious indulgence. The filthy black and silver stem was completely charred from so much use.

I pinched a rock from the little baggie and went to work. *Kerpow!* On that first hit, I realized the shit from old Carl was something special. The rush was entirely orgasmic. For hours I lay on my bed; propped up against the cold, clammy wall feverishly smoking smoking smoking until it was all gone.

After the pipe cooled, I heated and inhaled the crystalline residue remaining on the inside shaft and bulb. As soon as that was depleted, I tore open the tiny zip-lock pouch like a skilled surgeon and extracted the powdery remnants of white and pink flecks nestled in the creases and folds of the plastic, and smoked that, too.

Deteriorating into a shivering, tongue-clicking, jaw-grinding mess, I attempted to rise from the bed. Viciously, my head swirled and the room spun into a blurred vortex. *Plop!* I fell onto the musty carpet. Although I succeeded in propping myself onto one elbow, it was a futile effort. I couldn't get up. I lay there as time raced by like a sped-up film.

I realized I had to work that evening. The thought which pounded in my fried brain was: I couldn't be late. I'd never hear the end of it from that bloated asshole Bob. I kept track of time from the various television programs which faded in and out from the living room on the set I had forgotten to turn off.

"Today on Oprah Winfrey!" It's 3pm. No worries - I didn't have to be at work until eleven. I squinted out the unbearably bright window. The tree outside morphed into obscene Disney characters. The undulating leaves a translucent, neon green. I looked on, transfixed in terrified, paranoid, fascination as animated ducks, dogs, and mice grimaced mockingly back at me.

"Live from San Diego - It's Chanel 5 news at five!"

Okay, it was 5pm. My peeled eyes darted uncontrollably about the room. I had shortness of breath and was still completely paralyzed.

The *Star Trek* theme began. It was six. I felt as if I was about to blackout. I twitched and shuddered in a vain attempt to at least sit up from my fixed position as that galactic aria accompanied by bongos wailed on.

The boinging tune of *The Simpsons* popped on. It was seven. I needed to get up and get ready for work. As *The Simpsons Back to Back Comedy Hour* drew to a close. I thrust my torso upward - stood fully erect - naked - ultimately falling straight and solid as a board, swirling, and crashing onto my bed. I lay akimbo for a moment and burst into laughter.

If only this was caught on film, I thought.

As the *Law and Order* theme drummed on, I realized it was 9 o'clock and I had to get my ass in gear. Popping up once again, my body tingling and head swirling, I shuffled into the small bathroom and splashed water onto my greasy face. I wasn't in there long, that water hurt my skin.

Dressed, I darted out of my apartment into the cool night and hailed a cab at the corner. Reaching downtown Tijuana, I made my way to the border.

I felt fantastic. Everything was in sharp focus, every sound crisp and clear. Rapidly crossing a pedestrian bridge which spanned the sewage-crusted Tijuana River, I gazed up into the night sky and the blanket of dark, pendulous clouds was outlined in strobing waves of purplish light. I smirked as I realized I was truly fucked up.

I passed two Mexicans on the wide, concrete bridge as they dashed in the opposite direction at supersonic speeds. Both were tweekers – dirty and furtive. They gave me knowing looks as our eyes met.

"White boy tweeeeeekin'!" One smiled.

I returned an appreciating grin and loudly exhaled as I continued my power walk up to customs.

Passing through Immigration without a hitch, I jumped the trolley to downtown San Diego. I glanced at my watch - 9:45pm.

Enough time for a quick beer, I mused.

The area in which I worked lay on the fringes of skid row. Trash-lined streets with old liquor stores and porno shops and cut-rate hotels. The throng of deviants who prowled the night were out in full force.

Junkies squealed and meth addicts howled at the big, yellow moon as prostitutes of both sexes did their orchestrated ballet back and forth in front of the Rialto Theater. Florescent shadows played along cracked walls.

"Hey, man - ya lookin'?" A white boy in dollar store hip-hop drag asked through crooked teeth.

"Nah, I'm cool." I kept walking.

Dark streets packed with filthy, tattered hobos lay in their own piss, and well-dressed, hip blacks on the hustle, clenching crack rocks in quivering, cold hands dominated the carnival atmosphere.

I stealthily pass liquor stores and blue red purple neon of porno shops which peddled it real nasty all night with all kinds of sick junkies screaming from the back alleyways of the world.

I walked along the discolored, spotted pavement and found a bar full of hip kids and fags. I sat there at the counter savoring my beer when a middle-aged black man - tall and rail thin - barged in and sized me up as an easy mark. He plopped next to me on a stool and began gesticulating with oversized, boney hands.

"Now, what you need is a safistamacated woman." He breathed liquor and halitosis into my face.

I glanced indifferently over to him and croaked, "What?"

"A safistamacated woman, boy. One'll fuck ya all night." When he said 'all', his yellow eyes rolled around a bulbous, ashy head.

I mumbled fuck off or I don't have time for your stupid shit or something equivalent and he stared me down all gangsta and shit, but opts to jet, leaving me to my beer. I quickly finished up, paid the man, and headed to work.

8

At the porno theater, it was another night of slithering predators, horny military, and crazed-eyed, twitching junkies. I was relieved I had the following night off. Good thing, too, I agreed to be a guide for two good friends visiting from my old home of Los Angeles.

After my shift, I checked my two associates in at the Gateway Hotel, a cheap and run-down building a few blocks from the international border. The hotel was built at the beginning of the twentieth century and it showed. I sat back on the squeaking bed in one of the hotel rooms and took a long drag off my cigarette.

My fellow Los Angelinos, who so graciously decided to drive down to visit, were Edison Diego, an extremely, intense man who held aspirations of being an independent filmmaker. Though heterosexual, he was gay-friendly, and brought Velveeta Jones with him, a four hundred pound Filipino drag queen with Down syndrome. What a pair.

Edison had gone to the corner market for more booze and I waited in his room.

I inhaled another drag, staring at the dusty fan slowly revolving up on the high ceiling. The pink walls were shedding and the toilet leaked constantly. My bottle of Jose Cuervo on the end table was nearly empty. Somewhere down the hall, a couple of stout housemaids babbled away in Spanish as *Rings of Fire* by Johnny Cash crackled over the AM station from the cheap radio on the dresser.

At that moment, someone gently knocked on the door.

"Yeah? It's open." I knew who it was.

The door creaked open and Velveeta entered the room. She was dressed in a tight tube dress of black and grey horizontal stripes, completing the look with bright red pumps and a ratty, bouffant black wig. Velveeta was a huge, dumpy trannie. The flat, mongoloid face, heavily made-up, accented the demented visage.

I grinned through bloodshot eyes, "Shit, girl! You look like a Mexican whore."

"Thanks. That was the look I was going for." Velveeta coyly stated, faking a big showgirl smile. She clopped over and retrieved the bottle of tequila from the nightstand. "I see you've been fucking your buddy Jose Cuervo?" She studied my body sprawled out on the bed. "You're drunk?"

"Don't get any of them queer ideas," I said sarcastically as I tried to get up.

"Don't flatter yourself, sweets. Not in the market for limp-whiskey dick at the moment. Anyway, we have to go get Edison." Velveeta extended her chunky hand to assist me. I grabbed her plump forearm and pulled myself off the bed. "It's almost time to meet Fat Charlie at the restaurant."

"Let's go, then," I said, fumbling through my pockets for the car keys.

Edison owned a clunker Fiat and I was the designated driver. I acquired a massive headache and made a mental note to pop the

Tylenol which was stashed in the glove compartment.

"Are you okay to drive?" Velveeta asked as she watched me wobble.

"Yeah. Sure...I'm fine." I declared, belching into my fist. I was lying.

Truth was, I was feeling a little sick. It had been at least twenty-four hours since I had taken a hit of anything and my muscles ached.

It didn't matter, in a few hours I would make a beautiful score, a veritable motherload. I relished in the fact I would be soon smoothed out free and gratis from Edison's fat wallet.

"I have a bad feeling." Velveeta moaned. "We shouldn't do this. This doesn't feel right. I've never been to Mexico and they say that city is dangerous!"

They who? I inwardly frowned.

"Oh, quit your whining, and let's go." I stepped out into the hall and grinned. "Don't worry, Big Mama, you're with me."

"That's comforting." Velveeta said sarcastically as she closed the door behind her, and followed me to the elevator.

We ran into Edison in the lobby. He looked like an emaciated Jack Nicholson on a three day coke binge, 40ish, and a junky. He wore an olive blazer with a black knit shirt and black slacks. Thinning, brown hair was slicked back.

"Ready, kid?" He asked as we clopped out of the elevator.

I noticed he was empty-handed.

"What happened to the booze?" I inquired.

"Stupid chink bitch at the store said I was too intoxicated to sale me any." Edison grimaced. "Who the fuck she thinks she is? I'm an American. My money's not good enough for her ugly, Chinese ass?"

"Let's go." I sighed.

We stopped to pick up Fat Charlie. A monstrous, bear of a man. Obscenely bloated in torn, ragged clothes with a cherub face perpetually stuck in a silly, demented smirk - even when he was upset - and the permed mullet did not soften that grizzled appearance.

Fat Charlie was well known among the skid row sect of San Diego. His chubby digits were firmly placed in all sorts of nefarious illegalities: from the selling of drugs (notorious crack head, he) to the trade of hot merchandise, and the embezzlement of food stamps. Not a vicious, arrogant man - unlike most addicts – on the contrary, he was quite jovial and fun to be around.

Fat Charlie was a junky regular at the theater. One night as we shot the shit at the concession window. He stood enthusiastically licking orange Cheeto residue off of his dirty fingers like a giddy child.

I leaned against the file cabinet, smoking a cigarette, "Hey, Charlie, ever been to Tijuana?"

"Border's pretty hot." He belched like a foghorn while rubbing his obscene, bulbous stomach. "Once in a while, I get down there for some of that el cheapo booger sugar. Know what I mean?"

I ignored the wafting stench of his Cheeto-laced halitosis, "Well, I got two friends coming down from L.A. and they are in the market for a large amount of coke. Thought I'd play tour guide and show them TJ. You wanna come?"

Fat Charlie casually ripped open the depleted bag of Cheetos and began licking the inside lining like the cooch of a two-dollar hooker, "How much we talking about?"

"A lot." I continued. "We are meeting my contact down there and he promised to hook us up and cheap."

"Cheap? I like cheap. Yeah, count me in. I could definitely restock my supply."

Edison, Velveeta, and I met Fat Charlie at the border on the San Diego side. Fat Charlie jumped into the car and we headed toward the frontier.

Velveeta was excited, she never had been to Mexico before and repeated that bit of information every few minutes.

As the sun began to set, I drove the brown Fiat across the international border without being held up at the Mexican checkpoint. The uniformed official casually waved us through, not even glancing at the car.

"I guess they'll let anyone into Mexico." Edison observed as we maneuvered into downtown Tijuana. The traffic was dense and unbearable.

"Where the fuck is this place?" Edison grunted.

"We're almost there, Buckaroo, keep your cool," I said, noticing his agitation.

"Wow! Look at all the Mexicans!" Velveeta noted on the pedestrian view of the downtown area.

I pointed towards a nearby corner, "There should be some parking spaces next to that old church."

We circled the block. I had problems finding a parking space, the congested traffic was expectantly horrendous.

Eventually, I parked next to the old cathedral on 2nd and Avenue Niño's Heroes, a pile of ancient stone which dated back a couple of centuries.

Our group exited the car.

The sidewalks bustled with people; all dashing to and fro in their various affairs. Lingering next to a bronze statue of a pigeon-dung-covered saint was Mario, looking bored in his cholo street clothes. Mario was our contact on this deal. We casually greeted each other and the world seemed a little bit better to me now that I was with him. His dark eyes - always shrouded in lanks of hair - were already lit.

Sticking out like a group of retarded tourists, we were swarmed over by taxi drivers all on the hustle:

"Downtown, Meester?"

"Pussy women? Titty girl?"

"Donkey Show?"

"Best pussy...no like pussy? I got boys...twelve years old!"

"Oh God", Edison groaned. "I gotta get some smokes."

He made his way towards a couple of boys selling cigarettes at the base of the missions' steps.

Good ol' Mexico, I thought.

At that moment, three little children, two boys, and one girl - dressed in rags with dirty, bare feet – timidly approached Velveeta with outstretched hands, and smiled.

"Oh," Velveeta cooed. "How adorable! Here you go." Velveeta smiled, giving each kid a dollar.

"I wouldn't do that," I warned.

As if on cue, dozens of kids and men approached her with palms outstretched.

Mario yelled at the growing mob, waving his hands, *"Oye! Vete de aquí ya!"* (Hey! Get out of here, now!)

The group moved sullenly away.

Nearby, there was a public telephone. Without saying a word, Mario walked up and plugged a few pesos into the machine. He began speaking in Spanish to someone on the other end.

An old man in a grey, dirty jacket - shiny over the dirt - approached Edison with a cardboard box containing a variety of different brands of cigarettes.

Edison pointed at a pack of Lucky Strikes and asked the street vendor. "How much?"

"*Veinte pesos.*" The man said.

"What's that? Two dollars?" Edison asked.

"Yeah. More or less." I interjected.

"*Si. Dos dólares.*" The old man smiled and took the two and crumpled bills. "*Gracias.*"

"Yeah...grashiass...Hey, Mario, where's this friend of yours?" Edison impatiently asked, ripping open the package of cigarettes.

Mario continued for a couple of minutes on the phone in Spanish and then hung up the receiver. "Okay, I told him to meet us at Villa Garcia. It'll be about thirty minutes. Let's go."

"Where's this place at?" Edison asked with suspicion in his voice.

I pointed across the street, "See that row of shoeshine booths? It's right around from there."

We crossed the busy street and turned the corner into the plaza.

On weekends the plaza was packed with hustlers cruising for a few bucks. This was the meeting place for all the local men who wanted an afternoon diversion.

Under the blazing sun, teeming flesh eyed one another with unbridled, macho lust. After the sun went down, the hustlers were a bit more seasoned and professional.

I glanced at a young Mexican boy who looked back and smiled, I confided in Edison, "You know, when I first moved to Tijuana, the thought of paying for sex appalled me. My misguided, American attitude was that I was looking for love and not sex. Guys should love me for who I am and not for what I have. Right? This is a vulgar lie. In the gay life, there is no love...only sex. And for the most part, a dull disappointment. So, during my exile from the Land of the Free and the Home of the Brave, I have come to look at the sex act as a commodity of necessity. One which could be purchased not unlike a pair of shoes or a pack of cigarettes."

"I wish you knew my old lady," Edison stated as he took a drag off of his cigarette.

Next to a ruined arched wall at one end of the plaza, a group of performers dressed as Aztec Indians danced to a tribal beat. They were surrounded by locals and a scattering of curious tourists.

"Oh, why didn't I bring my camera?" Velveeta moaned.

Following Mario, our group eventually came upon a pair of old, swinging wooden doors painted a vibrant yellow.

I stopped and turned to the bunch, palm outward, "Well, here it is! Bar Villa Garcia!"

"Ahh...booze." Edison sighed as he stepped in the door, removing his shades as the group followed.

Our eyes adjusted slowly to the dark of the low ceiling room. There were but a few, cheerless patrons in the cantina. They gravely sucked on their beers, not saying anything. A ferret-faced rentboy leaned against a jukebox eyeing us as we entered, lithe hand on his crotch, languidly rubbing his money maker. A fairy and a gangster sat in a booth. At intervals, the fairies high cackle drowned out the bleating tune on the jukebox.

We filtered toward the back of the bar and sat on dented, wobbly stools. One of the washed-up whores who tended the bar approached us.

Squat in stature, she was a heavily made-up old woman with short, blond hair. She looked younger than her actual years.

She approached Mario with an outstretched palm and a smile. They greeted one another in Spanish with a peck on the cheek.

"Oh," Velveeta complimented, "She is so pretty. I love her shoes. Are those cha-cha heels?"

Mario looked at everyone and said, "This is Sylvia. She's asking what you want to drink."

"Just order five caguamas," I suggested.

"What's a caguama?" asked Edison. He pronounced it ko-wamma.

"See those big bottles that look like forty-ouncers?" I said, pointing toward the other patron's large, brown bottles around the bar. "Those are called caguamas. Single beers cost almost the same. Locals order them to save money."

"And trust, we look like anything but locals." Velveeta twittered.

Edison watched the entrance nervously. The door swung open and a stooped man in black, tattered clothing shuffled into the cantina. He wobbled as he walked, obviously intoxicated. He shuffled passed Velveeta, flashing her a wink, and a toothless smile.

Though he stank of stale urine, Velveeta smiled and chirped, "Hi."

The wizened, old man continued his hobble into the mensroom which lay adjacent to where our group sat. Sylvia returned with our bottles and glasses. Serving them with lime slices and salt.

"Mmm, I feel right at home," I confessed with a perk. "This is my old stomping ground. I used to come here and pick up all the time. That restroom right there was a veritable bathhouse during the night. All manner of drug fueled crimes against nature would be committed. It would become so congested a line would form – and that wasn't simply to just take a piss. I do adore the romance of Mexico."

Like the others, I began pouring beer into a glass.

Edison glanced over to the mensroom. From his vantage point, he could see into the restroom with an unobstructed view of the urinal trough.

"Typical gay bar set up." Mumbled Edison. "Freakin' penis peepers."

From the restroom, in front of the urinal, the ancient and drunken street tramp smiled his toothless smile, a black hole surrounded by a wild mane of frizzy, white hair. His grin fixed on Edison, in one motion, the drunk pulled down his stained grey trousers and loudly, and abundantly, plopped a big shit into the urinal trough.

"Lovely," Edison uttered, face blank as a poker dealer. He took a big gulp of his beer.

Ignoring the crap show Edison was witnessing, I continued my rant to both Velveeta and Fat Charlie, though loudly enough for Edison to pick up what I was saying. "Yeah. The people down here are so cool. I never had a problem with them. Unlike Americans, you know? I've made so many friends in Tijuana and I mean friends for life! Americans themselves are a defensive culture. Mexicans, I believe, are more open and friendly. I don't know what the fuck happens to them when they go across to the States, though. They all turn so goddamn mean."

"Speakin' of friendly," Fat Charlie interjected, "Follow me into the mensroom, young man. I wish to talk to you."

I knew exactly what this conversation was going to be. I followed Fat Charlie into the mensroom. The old tramp wobbled out, patting my shoulder on the way, softly cackling. The room smelled unbelievably foul.

Fat Charlie entered the only stall, "Just a minute, young man, I'll be right out."

I waited outside the rusted metal stall as I listened to the distinct sniffing and snorting from Fat Charlie which could only mean one thing. I shifted from one foot to another as my junk cells snapped into overdrive.

I glanced down at the urinal trough which lined the opposite wall. On the far end of the pink-tiled trough, a mound of dark feces piled in the middle; a putrid, chocolate-colored stream flowed down into the grated drain trap.

The steel door of the stall swung open with a resounding clang as Fat Charlie exited the metal cubical. He winked at me.

His face distorted in that silly grin, said: "Please, step into my office, senor. Hold up - do I have anything showing?"

He lifted his head so I had an unobstructed view of his hairy nostrils; they were caked in meth and dried mucus.

"Nope," I said. "Nothing at all."

"Righty-oh!" Fat Charlie breathed.

As Fat Charlie returned to the bar, I entered the stall and noticed two huge lines of white crystal methamphetamine displayed across the top of the graffitied toilet paper dispenser.

With one fluid motion, I whipped out a single twenty peso note from my wallet, rolled it into a tube, and vacuumed the meth up.

I stood up straight. Habitually tilting my head back, snorting the drug into my sinuses. Wiping the residue off of the grimy dispenser with my index finger, I casually massaged it across my gums. The junk circuits in my mind began to pop and crackle to life as the drug took hold.

With twitching, spastic movements, I returned to the bar where Velveeta and Fat Charlie were whispering secrets to one another and giggling like High School confidantes as I took a seat.

I looked at the two, asked, "What?"

Edison lit another cigarette and turned to me, ignoring Mario, who was having an animated conversation with the bartender, Sylvia.

Edison looked around, "You know, I bet it wouldn't cost much to open a bar here. How much do you think? Three? Four thou?"

"Would it be a gay bar?" I spat tensely.

"Ah fuck no! I'd make it a swanky joint and fill it full of slot machines and young, female hookers! Ya know, fifteen, sixteen years old. Of course, those little bitches'll have to sleep with me to get the job." Edison took a puff from his cigarette.

"You'd have to pay the cops off. Especially for something that crooked." I stated and grabbed a lemon, squeezing a few drops into his beer.

In my time south of the border, I had to sit countless of hours in as many bars listening to expats wail on about how they are going to move to Mexico and set up shop. A hopeless dream. What is it with westerners and their arrogance of wanting to slink into a country and think it was simple and without problems to open a bar or casino or whorehouse without difficulty? Stupid, really.

Velveeta and Charlie began laughing as both rose from their stools and walked into the restroom.

At that moment, two men entered the cantina. The obvious leader of the duo was in his early fifties. He was tall with salt and pepper hair. The thick mustache was dark grey. He was in good health and handsome for his age; not a wrinkle on his solid, masculine Latino face. He had black slits for eyes. Well-groomed and dressed, he sporting a mustard suit with a white t-shirt under the buttoned blazer. A gold chain hung around his thick neck which read *HECTOR*. His black, shiny boots clacked as he walked with confident deliberation.

The man was flanked by his lackey; a short stocky Mexican in a white tank top and dark brown chinos with body a mass of scars and tattoos. These were Mario's friends, and our connections.

Mario introduced the older guy as Hector and the other I did not catch his name. Hector asked Mario into the mensroom and a deal was made. Eventually, the two exited and approached Edison.

"You want coke?" Hector asked with a stoic machismo.

"Yeah."

"What else you want?" Hector rumbled.

"Whatcha got?" Edison smoothly asked as he took a gulp of his beer.

A sly smirk appeared across Hector's face, "You got money?"

"Enough." Edison snorted.

Hector motioned to Edison with two fingers, "Come with me."

For the next six hours, it was a drunken and dope-fueled party of brightly lit tableaus and a candy-colored kaleidoscope of broken images: Whorehouses, seedy bars, a macho goose in a doorway. Faces hidden in darkness and confusion. A whore with clown makeup winked so nasty. Smoke. Reggaeton blasted over speakers. Cocaine was bought. Piled into a taxi. Weed was bought. Walked through evil, dark barrios. Crystal was bought. Large amounts of liquor were consumed. A sinister midget laughed through silver-capped teeth. Smoke. Flashbulb of light. *Mucho machismos.* Edison howling drunken insults at the natives. Fists and knives were presented. *Whack! Pound. Pound.* Pound into someone's head. An Angel fell a victim. Crack of bones and a fairy screamed. My friend was swarmed over, a dark mass of fists and kicking cowboy boots. Smoke. Flashing light. Light gleamed on a knife and a friend went down in a pool of black blood and spit. Silver teeth revealed through snarled lips, "*Vamanos, gringo.*"

Dragged across flagstones as reggaeton wailed. Shoved into a taxi and sped off into the night. Air filled with the smell of burnt oil and marijuana.

Coffee was shoved under my nose, pills placed into my mouth. I looked up to see Mario wiping a wet and bloody hand towel across my forehead with red and scraped knuckles. He lit a Lucky and placed it on my lips. Blood trickled out of his nose, past his split lip.

Glancing around, I was back home.

"Damn. That was close." I croaked.

Mario's smirking face filled my vision, "Just another night in Tijuana, eh, *guero*?"

9

Jose Perez and I briskly walked through the Old Mercado in central Tijuana. The Mercado was a section of small streets lined on both sides with bazaars. Merchandise and Mexican curios overflowed onto the dirty, cobblestone lanes. A train of burros loaded with goods blocked our way. I pushed through, twisting my body sideways, squeezing past people. The hot wind blew little eddies of dust and trash into the side doorways.

A native of Ciudad Juarez in the Chihuahua Desert, Jose was a tall, thin boy in his early twenties. Coffee-colored skin and a smile that melted hearts. Blessed with curly, black hair he kept shortly cropped and penetrating hazel eyes, he was strikingly handsome. At one point he did confide wanted to be a model.

However, it seemed his guardian angel fell asleep at the watch. With a little persuasion from his friends, Jose had become a full-blown junky.

Since the death of his parents, he worked for his uncle who was connected with one of the major drug cartels of Northern Baja. He assisted his uncle on various occasions smuggling a fair amount of illegal drugs across the border. Since he was never apprehended by the officials, Jose carried that air of unstoppable, youthful arrogance.

In the bustling market, Jose and I passed the various stalls which sold all types of curios and toiletries, weaving through the throng of people until we came upon a worn-out metal gate.

Six tired-looking and slightly obese Mexican whores stood in the white-washed entrance with bored, sad looks upon their heavily painted faces. Above the door hung a sign in English: *HOTEL PARIS: NICE GIRLS, CLEAN ROOMS.*

A pudgy prostitute clawed at me and hissed, "*Psst, psst.* You wanna fuck me, *gringo*?"

"Not today, Esperanza." Jose smiled, pushing her aside as we continued rapidly down the clammy hallway and into the decrepit hotel.

The general ambiance of the lobby was dank and filthy. The tattered furniture and the foyer stank of cigarette ash and urine. The paint was flaking off the yellow walls as a radio blared Mexican top 40. The commanding view from the large window at the registration desk was of a canal backed up with last month's sewage. Atop fetid, murky waters, yellow feces slowly swirled in the sun.

Four spandex-clad whores sat in the corner on an overstuffed, blue couch with the grungy foam bursting out, waiting under the red glow of Christmas lights strung up in the corner. They sat quietly with that bored look on their faces as all whores do.

A prehistoric hag sat behind the desk. Dressed in a flowered, old frock, her face was plastered with so much makeup it took on the characteristics of a kabuki mask. She lit a dark, brown cigarette in trembling, gnarled hands. Her boney fingers were yellow from the nicotine. She eyed me with overt suspicion as if I had raped her virgin daughter.

To her left stood a hulking Mexican named El Chivo. A human tank. El Chivo remained motionless in dirty t-shirt and jeans. His thick arms folded across a barrel-shaped chest.

From behind wraparound sunglasses, bloodshot eyes watched us as we entered the lobby. El Chivo's faded, red t-shirt read, *Where's the Beef?*

Jose stopped and hugged the old lady, "*Hola, Senora Alma.*"

"*Hola,* Pepe, is everything good?" The old woman croaked.

"*Si, Senora Alma.*" Jose gave a curt nod to El Chivo and both exchanged a street-wise handshake. Jose motioned to me. "This is my friend. He is an American living in TJ."

Alma extended a withered hand covered in liver spots and as I shook it, her bones rattled. "You are always welcome here, *gringuito.*"

"Thank you." I smiled.

Jose glanced around. "Have you seen Gabriel?"

Alma took a long and heavy drag from her cigarette and pointed toward the ceiling with thick, black-lashed eyes. "He is in his room."

Jose and I climbed the rusted, spiral staircase into a dank corridor littered with garbage and dog shit. Somewhere from down the hall blared *No Sympathy for the Devil* by the Rolling Stones. From one cubical emitted the muffled moaning of a whore earning her rent.

At room twenty-six, Jose tapped on the gnarled, green wooden door.

With a series of clicks, a scrawny whore named Maria answered by cracking the door open. Her black hair was a wild and matted frenzy and her skull-like face painted up with red lipstick, smeared. Her front teeth stained and capped with silver. She stood there staring at Jose; eyes unfocused.

"*Hola,* Maria," Jose said, attempting to look past her ratted hair. "I'm here to see Gabriel."

Without waiting, Jose pushed past Maria into the room.

The hotel room was small with flaking, graffitied walls painted avocado green. The room contained a black chest of drawers and a couple of old, wooden chairs. The faux leather seats were cracked and full of slashes. Blue milk crates supported a small, black and white television which never worked. Commanding the room was a large, black-iron framed bed, and next to the bed lay a small, wooden table that had been hand-painted yellow. On the stained ceiling, a fluorescent light fixture flickered with the death throes of moths within. As with the rest of the hotel, it smelled of mildew and cigarettes.

On the worn-out bed of ratty and discolored sheets lounged Gabriel, an emaciated junky in his mid-forties. His forearms a mass of scar tissue covered in crude prison tattoos. His white tank top was spotted with blood and mucus and his khaki chino pants stiff from not being changed in months. A thick mustache covered full lips which were drawn downward in a grimace of petulant annoyance. The brown eyes sparkled with an inner fire.

On the rickety table next to Gabriel sat his works: a hypo, glass of tepid water, cotton balls, a blackened spoon, and a pack of black tar heroin. He swung his legs off the sagging bed and sat up; looking past Jose.

"Maria, go get some flautas from Tito. I want to talk to Jose for a moment." Gabriel hung there for a few seconds, stroking the long and black shiny hairs which drooped over insipid lips, and then stated, "It's about time you got here, Pepe, I got a job for you."

"For reals?" Jose said to Gabriel.

He sat down on a chair next to Gabriel and lit a joint which sat festering in an ashtray overflowing with cigarette butts.

"I just got off the phone with Gordo Bastardo. That *pinche gringo* wants to buy some shit offa me. I need you to run it over to him." Gabriel took the joint from Jose and inhaled a long drag. "You're Tio will pay you when you get back from the States."

"Hell, yeah." Jose agreed, coughing up the smoke and waving it away with his hand. He then nodded in my direction. "My friend wants to buy a dime of crystal."

Gabriel stared indirectly at my chest and whispered as if asleep. "Crystal? Wants to buy crystal?" He snapped back into focus. "How much you want to get, *guero*?"

"A dime will be fine," I said flatly. The guy creeped me out.

Gabriel reached into the small, yellow end table next to the bed and retrieved a plastic bag with fifteen or more little baggies of methamphetamine in it. The bag was wrapped closed with a rubber band. He unsnapped the band and withdrew a small, zip-lock baggie. Gabriel casually took my money and handed me the dope.

"Thanks," I said.

Gabriel smiled; the two front teeth were missing. He removed a blue bandanna from his back pocket and calmly wiped the sweat from the back of his neck. "Jose, be careful with these *gringos*, don't trust them. They destroy everything they come in contact with."

Jose took another hit off of the joint. "Hey, *compa*, it's me...remember?"

"For reals, ese." Gabriel then reached over and fingered the heroin in the aluminum foil package. He gave a sly glance toward Jose. "Wanna take a hit?"

Jose's eyes took on a dreamy gaze. "Yeah."

"Be careful...this is some strong shit," Gabriel warned as he reached for the blackened spoon. He placed the heroin in the spoon and, flicking a lighter underneath, cooked it down.

Drawing the solution through the cotton with the hypo, Gabriel stood up and gazed into the frosted mirror on the wall. The mirror bore a multitude of soccer team stickers surrounding the wood frame.

With a jab, he plunged the needle into a vein of his neck. His breath hissed through clenched teeth. Gabriel stared at his reflection in the mirror. Death looked back at him. He slid the needle out. His face went slack as the heroin coursed through junk-hungry cells.

Gabriel staggered back and handed the syringe to Jose.

"Some good shit, eh?" Jose whispered.

As Gabriel lay back on the bed and exhaled his breath in a warm cocoon of comfort, Jose cooked up his shot.

With swift, experienced movements, he grabbed the bandanna from the table and tied up his right arm. Probing for a vein with his left hand, Jose jabbed the needle into his flesh and pushed the plunger down, watching the solution drain into his arm. A soft blow hit his heart and then spread through his body.

"*Orale.*" Jose sighed.

He staggered to the bed and lay next to Gabriel. Though his body was slack and immobile as a lizard resting on a rock, his mind raced with images of brightly lit tableau.

Jose glanced at me with a distant, dreamy look, and held out the syringe. "Hey, handsome, want some?"

"No." I refused, sitting at the rickety table; laying out a fat line of speed. "Not into needles, kiddo. Shoot your way to heaven."

Jose glanced over at his friend Gabriel and noticed he was nodded off in a nostalgic reverie. Jose stood up, but the gravity pull of junk overtook his weakened body. He slumped into a chair opposite the bed. He tied up for another shot. He had a problem hitting a vein and the needle clogged. A line of blood ran down his smooth, brown arm. Jose looked down at the blood running from elbow to wrist. Affectionately, he wiped the blood from his arm. He slid the needle in and pushed the bulb down. He felt the junk hit him all over.

Slowly, Jose's head wilted to one side and his tongue fell out. The syringe tumbled from his hand and rolled across the dirty, tiled floor. A gust of hot wind blew frayed, green curtains into the room.

I hunched over and took a long snort of meth off the table. I glanced over at Jose. I actually felt sad. I pitied him. *Sweet dreams, Jose. Sweet dreams.*

10

He looked like a pedophile. Ashen grey in colorless shirt and pants. Balding head, paunch, and squinting, shifty eyes. That predatory stare of your person which always ended at your crotch.

I walked into the office as he stood next to the register, munching on a deli sandwich. The room reeked of garlic and raw onion.

"Howzit goin', Bill?" I asked.

I couldn't care less about the old fucks mood. Truth was, I couldn't stand him. I'm certain he harbored the same about me. He grunted something to the fact he was okay and returned gazing blankly out the box office window into the blackness, slowly chewing like a cow with anthrax.

I sat in the old, blue easy chair and quietly watched porn as the last forty-five minutes passed ending his shift.

Bill mechanically went over his notes. He had an annoying habit of jotting long lists of inane bullshit to pass off onto me every night at the beginning of my shift. I stood and listened with bored indifference.

After ten minutes of that crap, Bill grabbed his backpack and shuffled out the door to go wherever Bill goes at night.

I sat at the box office window on the rickety stool for a solid hour before I grabbed my notebook. I jotted down fleeting thoughts interrupted by perverts and junkies paying to enter the theater.

I reflected on my morbidly depressing, solitary life in which I had fallen. Ever since my relocation to Tijuana from Los Angeles, it had been one romantic letdown after the next. All crashing and burning from paranoid actions of my own design.

To be certain, I'd had my run of romantic relationships. In spite of that, I always found some surefire way of screwing them up. The drug habit certainly did not help. Sure, they gave me a thrill, they filled that void - nonetheless, I always returned to the same intersection of originality: Depressed and alone.

And yet, at the moment of contact - the exact moment when a random, love-struck fool was brave enough to open his heart to me - I became vicious and brutal. An arrogant monster, twisted in contempt and hatred.

Was it for the reason I had built up an impenetrable, emotional wall shielding me from that heart-shattering separation I fled from in Los Angeles? The old *'I'll hurt you before you hurt me'* routine? Or was it simply I wanted everyone who revealed the slightest interest in my well-being to feel the same vacuous pain I was burdened with?

I lit a cigarette and stared out the window.

Fuck it, I thought. *Leave that goofy shit for the psychoanalysts.*

I rose, locked the office, and headed towards the bathroom.

Passing through dirty, velvet curtains, I entered the main theater and marched towards the short hall to the right of the large screen.

I made my way past coughing, slurping, yawning, farting - I heard an old man gasp through a toothless mouth, "Itha cumin'!"

Quickly, I turned the corner behind the screen into a well-lit hall with red walls. A candy machine hummed as I noticed leaning up against the side, stood little Mario. He casually held a glass pipe to his mouth and his blowtorch lighter was blasting away.

He mocked surprise at seeing me, blowing huge plumes of grey smoke into the dank air.

"Hey, white boy! How's things?"

"Mario." I barely nodded.

"You look all sad and shit." He grimaced as he handed the pipe over to me. "Here, man - something to get this night going."

I took the pipe, it still being warm, and placed it to my mouth.

I stopped, eyeing him, "How much you got, Mario? I don't wanna do all your shit."

"Ah, dude," Mario stated casually as he flicked the lighter in front of me. "It's only dope."

Three hits later and I didn't even need to piss anymore. Mario followed me back to the office and sat in the recliner. I took the stool.

Mario pointed toward my open notebook next to him, "Watcha been writing?"

I shrugged and sighed, "Nothing of interest."

Reaching into the folds of his black, denim jacket, Mario stated, "Well, when you're a famous writer - remember me."

Why does everyone say that? I cannot (actually will not) wish to associate with any of these characters if and when I am a successful writer. And no junk for me!

Lounging on a tropical veranda in silk pajamas, sipping a martini, my every whim tended by a dark-skinned, exotic youth while I read my reviews in literary journals. Yep, I'll show them all!

But then again, that was the fantasy of an uncertain future. Now was now. And now, Mario was pinching more meth into his pipe.

He held it to his mouth, took a big hit, and passed it to me.

Thirty minutes later; we were spun. Twitching, shaking, sweaty messes. Mario sat hunched over in the chair. His dark eyes transfixed on the monitor which displayed a blond bimbo yanking a string of beads out of her butt by two sweaty Mexicans.

Mario leaned back and, with the concession door wide open, unzipped his black jeans, and pulled out his penis - completely erect - never had I ever witnessed that junkies junk that hard before.

"Damn," He quacked through trembling lips, "This makin' me hornier'n shit." His sparkling eyes darted over toward me. "You wanna?"

I hung the BACK IN 10 MINUTES sign on the concession door and closed it. Kneeling in front of Mario, I slobbered up and down on his long, dark penis until, with pointing of toes and quickness of breath, he squirted his semen into my mouth. I leaned over and - *splat!* - spit a bubbly wad of semen, saliva, and blood into the wastepaper basket.

I stood up and silently returned to the box office window. Mario zipped up his pants, fumbled with the front button. I looked at him, feeling cold and void.

Mario jumped up, "Whelp, going back into the theater. Here." He placed a tiny plastic bag in my perspiring palm. "This should keep you for a while. Laterz."

I mumbled thanks and later as the short Mexican darted out of the office and into the theater.

At that moment, the phone rang. Picking up the receiver, I heard the distinctive, labored breathing of obesity and knew exactly who it was before anyone answered.

"Is everything well?" The basso voice lisped.

It was Bob, the owner of the theater. He would occasionally call at odd hours throughout the night to make sure I was still there and not robbing him. He stated that fact openly a few times.

Bob also called in concern for his missing boyfriend. He and his lover - a potbellied, mustachioed queen named Keith - ran the theater with such totalitarian authority as only haughty fags could. Keith was prone to leave him and go on drinking binges for days or simply hole up in some bathhouse screwing his blues away. It was one of the missing Keith calls.

"Yeah, Bob, how's everything on your end?"

There was a pause, static, then the wheeze of someone who was suffocating under their own weight, "I want you to tell me, and remember...choose your words wisely."

Choose my words wisely? What the fuck does that mean?, I thought. *Fuck you, you fat bastard! Why does he have to annoy me with his woes concerning his infidel boyfriend?*

There was another deep gasp for air, "Have you seen Keith? Is he there?"

Fuck! I don't know, much less give a shit where that pot-bellied fucker's been spreading his gonorrhea. Let me get back to my dope!

"No, Bob, I'm sorry. I haven't seen him since yesterday when he was here with you."

There was a long pause. I heard wheezing. I waited, examining the grime under my fingernails.

"If he does decide to pay the theater a visit," Bob rumbled, "Call me, let me know."

I glanced at the wall clock - 2:38am. "Sure thing."

Click. I hung up the phone as two inebriated Navy men approached the box office window. One was a tall, thin Filipino - his eyes glazed and red from hitting the bars. His short friend was a blonde with tattoos on his forearms.

The blonde put his lips up to the hole in the window and slurred, "How much to get in, cowboy?"

"Six dollars," I stated.

The blonde glanced at his intoxicated buddy, "Wanna go in for a bit? Watch some nudie movies?"

The Filipino mumbled something unintelligible which made the blonde turn back in my direction, "Any bitches in there?"

I smiled coyly, "Oh, yeah...all kinds of bitches in here."

The blonde smiled knowingly, "No doubt. Gimme two tickets."

I took the admission and buzzed them in. I sat in the recliner and watched the porn drone on and on. I grabbed the now-tattered strip of aluminum foil with the meth Mario had given me and lit up.

Points in the room appeared into sharp focus. For the next hour, I dodged around the office meticulously inspecting every crack, every fleck of dust that lay about. Plopping back in the chair, I smoked more.

"Hey!" Called a voice from the box office window. "Hey!"

It was a short, shriveled junky. His face was sunken and unkempt. A scraggly beard partially hid the mass of festering acne on his neck. I noticed in those sparkling eyes, that he was lit up.

"How much, man?"

"Six dollars."

"Aw shit, dude - I ain't got six dollars." He whined dramatically.

I thought of my nightly supply and stated, "Right. You gimme a bump and I'll let you in."

He launched into the stupidity routine, "Bump? Watchu mean by that, man?"

"You know exactly what I mean," I stated dryly.

We stared at each other for a moment. He saw the raw sparks of tweek bursting in my eyes.

The junkie's face lit up with the flashbulb of addiction, "Yeah? Yeah! Awright."

I buzzed him in and he came around to the concession door. "You ain't no cop, right?"

"A cop working graveyard at a porno theater? You *are* suffering from paranoid delusions."

He reached down and dug into the crotch of his stained, corduroy pants, "Fuck. Can't be too sure, you know? Motherfucking cops everywhere nowadays. How long can I stay?"

"Until six o'clock when I close for clean-up. And, if you're nice - I may let you stay afterward so you can kick it all day tomorrow, too." I explained, watching him pull out a fat baggie of white powder.

He began that junky swaying con, "Well, don't you worry, homie - I'm gonna hook you up. Is this nice enough?"

"It's a start," I said smiling.

"Do me right, I do you right. Got it?"

"This'll be fine."

As he disappeared behind the musty, velvet curtains into the theater, I held the zip-lock baggie he had given me between thumb and forefinger. It was a fatty.

Without hesitation, I snatched my tattered and charred aluminum strip and went to work. I inhaled that sweet, metallic vapor through the melting straw. My lips began to burn - I smoked so much, so fast - I didn't care. My eyes stung and my breath quickened as I flopped into the easy chair.

Then, the damn phone rang. It was Bob. Same question - same answer. Through chattering, grinding teeth, I again assured him if Keith showed up, I would call. He hung up.

I sat trembling in the overstuffed recliner - transfixed, immobilized on the image of a black woman loudly slobbering up and down a bald stud's long cock. Then, to my left - *taptaptap.*

Looking up, it was the Filipino Navy officer who arrived earlier with the blonde serviceman. He swayed - eyes shifted from me to the porn on the monitor.

"Hey, man. Are there any strip clubs around here?"

I twitched, "Nope. None open this late."

"Really? Shit - what time is it?"

I didn't answer or look at him. I simply swung my arm up and pointed toward the wall clock. He stood there, leaning over the counter on his elbows, mouth ajar, and gaping at the porn flickering. A full minute passed. He snapped back into focus and pulled a small bottle of whiskey from his pant pocket, took a gulp.

He breathed liquor and stale peanuts into the office, "Wanna sip?"

"Sure," I said, coyly.

He handed me the bottle. The liquid burned going down my gullet, warming my stomach. He remained staring at the video on the monitor. His bloodshot gaze fazing in and out.

I simply wanted to get back to my dope. I darted my eyes up to him - not bad. Tall, well-defined torso, thick black hair, full lips, bloodshot eyes. He stood there, slack-jawed, pouty mouth hung open, shiny and moist.

On the monitor, the actress continued her rhythmic sucking and slurping. She huffed and moaned, casually smiling towards the camera behind heavily made-up eyes.

"Fuck! Goddamn!" The serviceman at the concessions door blurted out, "We need some bitches here, I want a blow job."

"Well, it's real late. No one here but me. Sorry."

"Damn, I need my dick sucked."

Mechanically, I stated, "Drop your boxers and I'll do it if you want it that bad, shipmate."

"What?!" He stuttered.

"Last chance."

"Shit. Don't hafta ask me twice." He entered the office, closing the concession door behind him.

He glared at me with the look of a guilty little boy about to do something bad. The pants dropped and I gave him the bestest of the mostest. After ejaculating, he gave me the old *Don't Tell Anybody Speech* before darting back into the theater.

Don't worry, kid, I won't tell a soul.

11

The streets were still wet when I got off work. The snobbishly rich were out in the blinding, white sun of early morning walking their dogs. Scores of them. I had oft considered San Diego the dog walking capital of the country.

I darted around the corner and entered *Mr. Lee's Café*. A minute, hole-in-the-wall diner. The long, high ceiling restaurant was the last of its kind downtown. All other family-owned restaurants had gone out of business, replaced with high-end fusion eateries and condos in the name of urban renewal.

Lee's was owned by an ancient Chinese man and his wife. The eatery was quite popular with the hobo crowd. A plate of eggs, ham, toast, hash browns, and a coffee still ran you about two-fifty.

I entered the joint and the smell of grease and unwashed bodies wafted thick through the tight air. The café had a wooden and warped counter which ran the length of the room. A row of aluminum tubed stools lined the counter and there were beaverboard walls with hooks for hats and coats. In the dirty back kitchen, the fryer and grill sizzled overtime as Mr. Lee prepared various orders.

At one end of the counter, in front of a dusty, glass-pane window cluttered with yellowed, handwritten menus, squat a stooped and ragged man. His grey hair a tangled mane, bush of beard, layered and dirty clothes - he sat sipping his coffee, staring into nothing, listening to the tinny crackle of a small, portable radio attached to his wobbly, aluminum cart which occupied the entirety of his dreams and possessions.

The four others at the counter were sullen, ratty phantoms of the night streets. They, too, sat solemnly and sipped coffee or shoved yellow messes of breakfast into slobbering holes. No one looked up as I entered, except a bloated, black man with milky cataracts in his left eye.

With a loud screech of metal on dirty linoleum, I sat at the counter as Miss Lee asked for my order with weary apathy.

"Coffee." I croaked.

From out of a back storage room wobbled a massive, squat woman with long, straight brown hair and great, tumbling breasts which overlapped her bloated stomach. As she ambled to the back of the counter, her green eyes, hidden behind large, oval, horned-rimmed glasses, caught my glance.

She smiled genuinely, "Oh muh God! Haven't seen you in a while!"

"Hey, Darlene." I wheezed. "I been working and doin', you know."

I made a quick sniffing noise, grinning smugly.

With a dirty rag, she wiped the counter in front of me, "Well after you eat, why doncha head over to my apartment for a visit. I got something I wanna show you."

Ms. Lee placed the coffee in front of me.

I said to Darlene as I stirred in sugar and milk, "Sure. When do you get off?"

"At eleven this morning. I hafta take little Bobby for a haircut before our appointment with the CPS tomorrow. You wanna wait for me?"

I thought a minute. Took a quick sip of the bitter-tasting coffee. "Okay. I'll hang out at the mall and meet you back here at eleven."

I pointed at the pen-written menu plastered on the wall mixed in with a Buddha shrine. "And, I'll take a number three." Number three was the cheap breakfast mentioned before.

Darlene was a woman whom I met as I lay on the slab at the local blood bank. I used to sell my plasma for money to score dope. She was a chatterbox, but a good person. I never seen her mean or angry, just overtly preoccupied about her weight. During one of our long tirades at the plasma center, we confided with one another we were both methamphetamine addicts.

Her apartment building was located on the fringes of skid row. Darlene shacked up with her current lover - a gangly, snaggle-toothed tweeker named Frank. He would cook up messes of fantastic shit in their small kitchen as the two kids from a previous, hellish romance played on the floor in the living room.

A few months prior, I would hang around every day, scoring and partying with these two hillbilly tweekers. Running errands, keeping Darlene company while Frank transported his homemade speed all over the southwest.

Things went sour real fast. Unbeknownst to Frank, Darlene had acquired a romantic interest in me and freaked out when she found that I was queer. It hit her hard. Frank being the stereotypical, red-neck homophobe didn't help matters much either. After heated verbal confrontations with Frank, I dropped out of that scene. I had to admit though; I missed getting that free dope.

That was then and over time, I guess she held no hard feelings.

As promised, I met Darlene standing out front of Lee's Café smoking a cigarette. We hopped the trolley the few blocks up to her building - an ancient pile of red brick which served as low-rent housing for welfare recipients and ghostly elderly. We slowly crawled up the sagging, wooden staircase. Up six flights as the warped steps loudly creaked under her titanic weight.

The apartment was cluttered and musty. Overstuffed couches from the Salvation Army clogged the room. Wadded clothes, dirty dishes piled on every table, crumpled newspapers littered the dirty, green-carpeted floor - various objects lay about which gave the impression some large beast had trampled through. Everything was worn and second-hand, except for a shiny, brand new, fifty-five-inch flat-screen television that dominated the room.

I sat on one of the dilapidated couches in the corner, contemplating out the window. A warm breeze blew in ruffling the yellowed, laced curtains.

"Where's Frank?" I asked.

"He had to make a run to San Bernardino - he won't be back for another day or two, I guess," Darlene stated absently as she meandered into the kitchen. "Want some Pepsi?" She hollered back as I heard her open the fridge.

Returning to the living room holding two plastic glasses, Darlene passed me mine and smiled, "You wanna smoke?"

I looked into her plump face, all the junk cells in my body lit up. I felt a lift, the same anticipated feeling when you meet an old lover and you know you are going to have sex again.

I took the glass of soda, "Sure, Darlene. Whacha got for me?"

"Go into the kitchen, love." She smirked, falling into a green recliner that poofed dust out from the seams and groaned in disapproval.

I casually walked into the small kitchen and stopped in my tracks. Amid piles of dirty, greasy plates and crusty utensils, mounded up on the untidy dining table was an assortment of Sudafed pills, a collection of chemical bottles, hoses, and pressurized cylinders. It was Frank's meth lab.

One of the major problems with homemade dope was those crazy kitchen chemists often threw in a bunch of fertilizer and No-Doze and Sudafed and gasoline, and who knows what the hell else, and what you ended up with some seriously toxic shit.

As every addict knows, there are a couple of ways to make meth, and a plethora of easily attained ingredients can be used. Most of the elements in making the narcotic could be found right in the home and be cooked and ready in six to eight hours in makeshift labs. It cost about $50 to $140 to make one ounce which can then be sold for as much as $1200.

Some examples of chemicals used to produce meth included, but are not limited to: Ether - Benzene - Methanol - Methylene Chloride - Trichloroethylene - Toluene - Muriatic Acid - Sodium Hydroxide - Table Salt - Ammonia - Pseudoephedrine - Hydrochloric Acid - Drain Cleaner - Battery Acid - Lye - Lantern Fuel - Anti-Freeze - Anhydrous Ammonia - Red Phosphorous - Iodine and whatever other crazy crap that could be thrown in.

In lieu of any fumes or vapors which were associated with the making of the narcotic, the cookware could be quickly relocated to avoid detection from the law without much of a hassle. However, most cooks don't bother and leave their gear behind. Makeshift labs abandoned become potentially explosive when the highly toxic contaminants were left to ferment.

Those lingering mixtures could cause nausea, headaches, dizziness, skin burns, and eye irritation. It affects soil, groundwater, air, furniture, and structure materials, such as flooring, vents, and walls.

Many of the contaminants present when making meth were extremely harmful to humans or pets if the exposure was prolonged. Cases had been reported where children and adults who lived in a house or other structure where former meth labs had been set up, encountered serious health problems long after the lab had been deconstructed.

It is a well-known, tired fact the most commonly used chemicals to begin the meth-making process were over-the-counter cold and asthma medications which contain ephedrine or pseudoephedrine as mild decongestants or stimulants.

As I scanned the room, empty Sudafed boxes overflowed the small, plastic trash can in the kitchen. However, that wasn't what stopped me. Dominating the filthy counter was a dinner plate possessing a colossal pile of methamphetamine. It resembled a chunk of crumbling birthday cake. I had never seen so much tweek at once in my life. I began to shake, felt my heart ping.

"The aluminum foil is in the cupboard, dear - take what you want. Bring me a little, will you?" Darlene called from the living room.

I grabbed the box of foil and placed several large crumbs into a napkin; returned to the living room. Darlene was sitting there with her works laid out next to her on an end table.

With speed, I hated to snort it as I preferred smoking. I obtained a better rush and it didn't fuck up my nostrils. That gunky-tasting residue lodged itself in the back of the throat never appealed to me. Yeah, I know, what about the teeth?

It is a long-winded, boring fact the chemicals used in meth production will rot out the user's teeth. I guess I had been blessed with strong choppers and unlike many a junky acquaintance, I did keep up good personal hygiene. No meth mouth for me.

Darlene was a skin popper. She enjoyed jabbing a needle into her haunches, claiming there was no rush like it. Injection was a popular method, also known as slamming, but, as everything, carried serious risks.

The hydrochloride salt of meth is soluble in water and injection users may apply any dose from 125 mg to over a gram, using a small needle. This dosage range may be fatal to non-addicts. Not so for the experienced addict, who rapidly develops a tolerance to the drug. Injection users often broke out in skin rashes (called 'speed bumps') and infections at the site of injection were common.

To each their own. At that moment, I wasn't going to categorically analyze the matter, I simply wanted to get high.

The two of us went to work. I found an ink pen, popped out the ink reservoir, discarded it, and used the casing for a straw. Ripping off a two-inch-wide strip of aluminum, I creased it length-wise to get that preferred groove down the middle. Placing a nice-sized rock in the groove, I put the pen casing in my mouth, and lit the underside of the aluminum strip with my lighter.

Heated, the speck dissolved into mercury-like liquid, emitting grey resinous smoke. I tilted the strip downward, letting the liquid ooze along the groove, following with my straw, inhaling the wisping smoke as it crept.

Instantly, I felt that static charge as it rushed and pulsed from my lungs, up the spine, across the back of the skull, and to my forehead. I could feel the hairs on my head prickling. My heart pounded and my sweat-filmed body quivered as I flicked the lighter over and over and over again under the strip, mechanically following the liquid dope up and down, up and down, up and down.

Darlene placed some tweek in a blackened spoon. She held a lighter under the spoon until the meth dissolved. Grabbing a syringe, she sucked the liquid up with a needle.

Leaning to her side, she pulled down her black sweatpants which exposed her unappetizing person to my fucked up gleam. A mass of white skin glowed, pockmarked by acne and red puncture sores. The smell of dirty ass and vagina punched me in the nostrils.

She somehow found a vein in that plateau of rippled dimples and jabbed the syringe in, pushing down the plunger.

She pulled up her pants, sat back, and sighed, "So, this some good shit or what?"

I was shaking, hunched over my aluminum strip, feeling like a fat kid in a candy store. I glanced at her and curtly nodded.

Darlene chuckled, "Frank left me a lot - so do what ya want."

Oh shit, I thought.

When I finished the dope I had first brought out, I quickly returned to the kitchen and grabbed more - and more and more.

All day, Darlene and I smoked and shot that shit like there was no tomorrow. Eyes wide and aware, mouths grinding and chewing, our body's tweeking in jittering jerks. Darlene and I sat and joked and laughed, completely spun out.

She looked at me and realized how haggard I looked. "When was the last time you slept, sweetie?"

"I don't know – days?" I sputtered. White balls of saliva flew from my mouth.

"Why don't you go into my room and lay down - try to get some sleep." Her motherly instincts coming through. "You want some Benadryl to help you sleep?"

"No."

I stood up and made my way to the bedroom. A queen-size mattress lay in the middle of the room covered in rumpled, musty blankets. I took my shoes off and laid down.

Every tweeker will disclose that they have a distinctive habit when they are spun. A repetitive quirk. This varies from individual to individual - hearing voices, seeing shadows, random hallucinations, or whatever. Mine was hearing fucking.

As I lay in the bed, I distinctly heard the muffled sounds of someone having sex coming from the other side of the grimy, plaster wall.

Thumpthumpthump. I rolled over in acute agitation, placing my ear against the cold wall.

"Yeah! Oh God, yeah! Fuck me, baby!" Moaned some bitch.

Between gasps and lunges, the sound of a young man grunted, "Yeah! Take... all... that... dick, baby!"

I lay against the cold wall, twitching, and sweating, listening to the moans from the adjacent apartment.

Didn't even think of pleasuring myself. On this much tweek, my cock was shriveled to a useless nub. It must've been two hours I lay prone and listening with an attentive ear at that couple - funny thing was, in reality, on the other side of the wall, there was nothing. Six floors down to a parking lot.

The lustful hallucination eventually became quiet as I adjusted myself into a more comfortable position. My mouth chewed and my teeth ground. I gazed out the window.

The sky was a harsh, bright blue, and the trees a vibrant green that swayed slowly in a breeze. With disdainful horror, the trees began morphing into Disney characters - a duck, a mouse, a dog.

I smiled, thinking, *Damn, this is some good shit.*

Hours passed and I could not sleep. I popped up off of the bed and returned to the living room. Darlene was sitting there twitching, holding a cup of coffee in one hand, with her syringe resting on the arm of the chair.

"Did you get any sleep?" She asked.

I sat on the couch, and grabbed the strip of aluminum, "Nope."

Flick whoosh!

"You gonna work tonight?" She croaked.

"No," I said, exhaling smoke. "As a matter of fact, I'm off."

Leering, she smiled coyly, "So, you wanna stay the night here?"

I continued smoking dope, not looking up, "I can't. I have to get back to Tijuana. I hafta do something."

She looked at me hurt. Darlene took a sip of her coffee as I inhaled the rest of the dope. I put the aluminum strip on the end table and sat listening down into myself. Long moments of awkward silence passed. Only the faint hum of the world reverberated in my skull.

I needed to get some sleep. My entire torso felt doughy, gummy, exhausted. Blanketed by the electrical charge of exhilaration from the drug coursing through my muscles. My eyes stung and my mouth tasted foul and evil.

A few moments passed, I blurted, "Darlene, can I take a bag with me? I'll get you back in a couple of days when I get paid."

"Of course." She sighed. She handed me a small zip-lock baggie. "Here. Go in the kitchen and grab what you want. But, I need you to pay me. Frank will get pissed if you don't."

In the kitchen, I filled the bag to the point of bursting. I gleaned the rim of the plate with a finger and brushed my gums with it. A tingling feeling washed over them.

I stood a moment, pondering the idea of shoving the rest of the dope on the plate into my pants pocket and simply bolting out of the apartment. Nah. I returned to the living room.

Darlene and I said our goodbyes and I walked the six flights down into the cool night. The stars twinkled and the traffic breathed. Jumping a trolley, I headed back to Mexico. I stood there in the back of the car, keeping an eye out for security.

Eyes shifted as the trolley rumbled, I glanced at the other passengers. I knew they were staring at me. What did they see? Was I that spun out I didn't fade completely into the shadows? Standing there in oversized, dirty jeans, a wrinkled sports shirt, a greasy, sweaty, pale face behind black, horn-rimmed glasses. I twitched and swung my head back and forth in mechanical clicks.

Obviously, I didn't care. All I thought was, I need to get some sleep.

12

I stood outside *Bar Ranchero* in the simmering night. The Plaza was pregnant with the twilight people.

Adjacent to my shivering form, the cantina thumped with laughter and merry-making. Inside, two old queens celebrated their *cumpleaños* - and they graciously flipped the bill for the posh and swanky fiesta. Crates of complimentary booze and mounds of vittles were gaily guzzled by nameless, arrogant faces.

I went into the bar for a bit - to be sociable, understand. I danced a little with a scrawny, attractive boy. He gyrated and swirled with lithe movements to the disco beat - what was his name? Who cares. I drank with vague, garrulous acquaintances. There were too many bodies that poured into the street, so I stood outside on that humid night and feigned interest with these faggoty-assed jerks.

By the entrance, Ivan - rentboy turned waiter, known him for years – strolled up and dramatically sobbed to anyone who would listen that someone had stolen all of his money. I leaned against a lamppost, lit a cigarette, and listened to Ivan go on and on about being ripped off.

How does it feel when it happens to you? I thought.

A big-boobed hooker clopped up to me as I stood watching Ivan's scrawny frame tilt and droop in overdramatic, drugged-out grief.

"Whacha looking for?" She asked.

"You don't got it - plus, I like men." I toked on that cigarette like a cock.

"I *am* a man." She quacked.

I took a closer inspection. Damn. The chick *was* a dude.

I knew then it was time to get out of there and quick. Go and search for some kicks elsewhere. Perhaps in Zona Norte. Hit up the park, maybe? Before I walked away, Ivan faded in and invited me to his trap. Why not? He was a good lay.

When I had first met Ivan, he was simply one of the legions of rentboys who hustled the Plaza. A young man of slight build, his copper-colored face was oval and almost Asiatic in appearance. He had high cheekbones and almond-shaped eyes. The one thing which appealed to me more than his slim and well-toned physique was his jet-black, wavy hair. I had always been a sucker for black, wavy hair.

"*Aye*, those *putos* took my money, *guero.*" Ivan whined.

"Yeah? That's too bad." I didn't care. With eyes shrink-wrapped in tears, he hit me up for one hundred pesos to make a score. "Sure, Ivan. Sure."

In the dark streets which led to his crumbling hotel, phantoms lurked and casually offered junk amid hushed hisses and probing fingers.

"Nope, I'm good," I muttered as Ivan copped a paper from one of those shadowy denizens.

We dodged around the corner to a shitty hotel. CONTINENTAL, the marquee read. Up a worn and wooden staircase, Ivan and I entered a small room only furnished with a bed and a squat bookshelf, dirty clothes wadded and crumpled on the shelves.

He took out a glass pipe from between the bare mattress, crushed the crystal into it, lit up, and smoked - billowing huge plumes of that grey, tinny smell. Ivan handed me the charred pipe. I faltered, internally reassuring myself that I could quit at any time.

One toke, two, three - we passed it back and forth in junky silence as if performing an arcane religious ritual.

Ivan degenerated into a shaking, teeth-grinding wreck. Within moments, and right before my eyes, his handsome face shriveled over his skull, the check bones stood out, the eyes wide open - peeled, raw. A face of death.

When the dope was gone, he stashed the blackened, glass tube under the stained mattress. He lay back with hands clasped behind his head and listened to ranchero music on his CD Walkman. His red t-shirt was lifted a bit, exposing the muscles of his brown abdomen. A line of coarse hair trailed from his belly button to his loose-fitted and dirty jeans.

I lit a cigarette as I sat on the edge of the bed, glancing around the dirty, pink walls as the tweek set in more on Ivan than myself. That acrid, heavy-metal taste lingered in my mouth which no cigarette could erase.

I studied Ivan with pity as he convulsed in mechanical jerks. He rose and dragged the bookshelf (cockroaches scattered) in front of the door. He wordlessly returned to his music. Safely barricading himself from paranoiac

Dream Police. Ivan retrieved his pipe again – expertly scraping the residue from the stem for another round. He faltered; eyes wide like an animal sensing danger.

"Hear that, *guero*? *Placas!*" He whispered as he placed a grimy finger up to his lips.

Outside, heavy boots and jingling keys passed the door as Ivan's schizophrenic paranoia flared. We sat a long moment in silence and waited for the stranger to pass.

I declined the second dose and had enough of this hopeless Fallen Angel. Once upon a time, he was strong and virile. Now, the mind was gone. At least the boy had retained his looks of strong, angular Aztec features. I sadly realized, soon that would decay.

I realized I wasn't going to get any sex tonight from this character. He was far too gone. I stood and extinguished my cigarette on the filthy, wooden floor.

"I gotta go," I mumbled.

Exiting the gloomy room, I left that wretch to his personal theater of horrors.

I walked the few blocks on that dark, humid night – keeping an eye out for patrols on account my own paranoia was kicking in. I thought of my future and my plans. I cannot allow these demons to control me.

Reaching my room, I undressed and lay in bed; unable to sleep as the drug took hold. Eventually, I drifted off and horrid nightmares abound. I woke up depressed as the urge of quitting my addiction festered in my mind. The cheap clock next to my bed read 3:26am.

I dressed and headed back downtown. The carnival atmosphere was still in full swing. I meandered through the Plaza. A whiff of meth drifted in the clear night, riding on the ranchero music. An old hag muttered over her candles and altars in a corner alcove of masonry. A mangy, white cat pulled at my pant leg and then ran onto a concrete balcony. The moon ominously floated by.

"Ivan!" Rentboys glanced up from card games, coffee houses, with sullen, hooked stances under metal light posts as the name echoed and slowly faded away. "Ivan! Saul! Diego! Jose!" Cries from a thousand faggots echoed on the warm night.

Ivan sat on a stool at the entrance to the cantina, *Villa Garcia*. With the flashbulb of recognition, his eyes lit up.

"Need you to do me a favor," I croaked, wiping away the more obvious signs of distaste with a waded, paper napkin. I noticed the yellow of meth on Ivan's face, "Don't ever invite me to do that again."

His body moved in little overanxious jerks as junk channels lit up. "Okay - okay. You certain?"

"I know what I'm doing." I breathed the residue of methamphetamine out of my already scarred lungs.

I walked alone down Avenida Revolucion toward my apartment amid the cavalcade of blaring neon and pounding discos. Barkers stood at every club entrance soliciting tourists and locals alike. Everyone looked like a drug addict.

I stopped to sit on a metal bench in front of *El Torito* disco. I wanted to sit alone and smoke a cigarette and think. My depression was rising again. I was awash in waves of despondent nostalgia from the adventure and wonder regarding my months in Tijuana. Nostalgic ferver which had soured and blackened over the years.

Moments passed and a handsome cholo pelon sat with me on the bench. From him wafted the smell of dirty linens and unwashed torso. We didn't talk. He catatonically gaped at nothing as he cackled and grinned into an overused Styrofoam coffee cup - he laughed, black insane laughter as patrol after patrol roamed past eyeing us.

This was too tiresome and I drifted home.

Lost without purpose or meaning, once again, I lay in my bed, naked, on top of the covers, smoking a cigarette. I watched a black cockroach scale the faded, baby-blue wall of my room, long feelers waving.

A national sponsored program in Spanish mumbled from the radio about catching crabs from prostitutes and I thought about my life, my habit, *I need to quit this shit.*

13

Jose Perez threw a party in honor of his new apartment. A two-room rat hole with a rusted steel balcony and a panoramic view of the Red Zone. Nice if you wanted to see smog, crisscross of wires, and bloated hookers clopping up and down the broken pavement.

But, ah yes, the aforementioned fiesta. All categories of sordid junkies and nefarious types lurked in the smoke-filled shadows of Jose's colonial trap. Cocaine, marijuana, speed, heroin, and booze passed many a hand.

Banda music boomed from a massive stereo system as the *vecinos* rushed about cackling like agitated jackals. I snaked my way through the pressing bodies and bumped into Ivan in the bathroom.

In a noiseless spotlight of inactivity, he stood like a faded, double-exposed photograph holding a glass stem in his trembling hand. With the mask of the damned on his ravaged face, Ivan regarded me with sick, brown eyes.

He sighed, "I'm killing myself with this shit, *guero*."

"Don't be foolish," I said coyly. "Plus, who wants to live forever?"

I took a hit or two myself and felt it.

"I'm a worthless fuck." He shook his head. "I'll be gone soon, *guero*. You'll see. I'll be gone."

With a look of hopeless finality, Ivan slumped silently against the green porcelain wall as I returned to the thumping revelry.

Half a bottle of tequila later and added effects of the tweek caused me to lose control. I stumbled and swayed in euphoria to the music. I got the terrors as I was surrounded by scores of grotesque, grinning faces.

My head throbbed from fatigue and I found myself in a dark corner in the hallway. I reached into my pocket and downed a handful of *asperina* with my beer.

Sniffing, I leaned against the chipped, lime-painted wall and listened to the hyped-up, drug-fueled patter of Jose as he gabbed garrulously in oscillating gestures to a ratty, sour-faced whore strung out on goofballs.

"...slammin' that *pinche chiva* with no electricity and only that red candle, ya know - they turned off all the lights and water months ago and I tell you, Pablito was happy to kick out that asshole roommate. There was garbage and shit and rats and roaches everywhere. *Huacala!* Never take a *pendejo* with a monkey, *mija*. You can't trust none of them motherfuckers. *No bueno.*"

14

The sky was that bright Mexican blue and the air was simmering humid. Mario and I darted into a filthy alley littered with broken beer bottles, syringes, and shit. Small children with dirty, bare feet played with a mangy dog.

We cut into a two-story hotel lobby at the dead-end of the blind alley. Passing through rotted French doors, I saw a fat *chilango* who sat behind the reception desk watching the flickering screen of a small, portable television. Atop the dusty, plastic set was an antenna crooked and ending in tattered wads of aluminum foil.

The receptionist swerved his head toward us with the look of a masturbating idiot. Mario and I approached the counter. The two exchanged greetings and the slobbish man mumbled something unintelligible.

Mario looked at me and nodded into the hotel proper, "C'mon, *guero*."

Passing through the dusty lobby which displayed old Spanish movie posters on maroon walls riddled with scribbled graffiti, we walked into the middle of the hotel's open courtyard. The building was old. It must have been constructed in the forties or early fifties. Warped, wood railings encircled the second floor with white paint curled and pealing. The loud cacophony of noises, from ranchero music to crying babies. permeated the stifling air.

Mario and I ambled over to a first-floor room. The door opened and as we approached, an old woman emerged.

"*Aei*, Mario! It is good to see you again." She cackled; arms outstretched.

Mario gave her a quick embrace, "*Hola*, Esperanza. Is Abel around?"

She flashed him a stern look, then called over her shoulder in Spanish, "Abel! You have visitors."

The frumpy hag stood unsympathetic and cold, grimacing at me with droopy eyelids. Arched eyebrows, as if they were scratched on with a magic marker, highlighted a ratty, orange wig that sat askew a prunish head.

"This is my friend. He lives here in TJ." Mario said solemnly.

Esperanza smiled like a predatory animal, exposing long and yellow false teeth.

She extended a gnarled hand, *"Bienvenidos, guero."*

"Hi." Was all I could say.

The sun hurt my eyes and I was tired. I hadn't slept in six days.

A voice quacked out from the back something to the effect that Mario should go there.

"Wait here," Mario mumbled.

I stood in the doorway as the short Mexican disappeared into the murk of the room.

My eyes adjusted to the gloom. There was an overstuffed, single bed with a ragged green cover. Clothes and knick-knacks were piled about. In a corner sat candles under a colorful altar to Guadalupe. A great deal of possessions were packed in bulging trash bags and brown paper sacks.

The old woman flopped onto a creaky, wooden chair adjacent to an old television. The seat squeaked loudly as she settled into her Spanish *novelas.*

Esperanza outright ignored me - hatred and distrust emanated from her shriveled and petit frame.

I know when I'm not welcome.

"I'll be outside smoking a cigarette," I muttered.

The old hag said nothing as she remained fixed on the television set. I silently walked outside.

I lit a cigarette and looked around. The cobblestone-brick yard was dotted with pools of dirty, incandescent water, rusted refrigerators, mop buckets filled with garbage - the stagnant air smelled of human waste and urine.

"Hey, white boy!" Yelled a voice from the second floor in English.

I ignored it.

"Hey, asshole! What the fuck you doin' here?!" Hollered the voice.

I glanced up to see an emaciated cholo in a worn, white tank top and dirty khakis with an oversized, black baseball jacket leaning over the balcony of the second floor. In his dark eyes raged searing hatred.

"What the fuck you doin' here?!" He bellowed again as he made his way along the railing toward the stairs. He kept those ferocious eyes fixed on me. "Get the fuck outta here! We don't want you here! Go back to your fucking country!"

"Yeah, I'm gonna do that just cause you told me to!" I shot back. I didn't flinch. I simply returned the macho fuck's harsh glare.

"What?!" His thin face contorted in hate. "What the fuck you say, motherfucker?!"

He quickened his descent as his hand reached into his tattered, stained jacket. My heart began to race. This asshole either possessed a gun or a knife and had every intention of using it.

"I'm gonna kick your motherfucking ass, you fucking cracker!" He bellowed.

I stood, clenching my fists, and retorted, "I'm right here, *naco*. I'm waitin'!"

As his first step left the stairs and onto the cobblestone, Mario popped out of the hotel room and stood there. My assailant stopped in his tracks.

A tense pause, then Mario said to me as he glared at the other guy, "Get inside. Abel wants to talk to you."

Mario led me past the unaffected old woman and into a back room. The pink-colored walls were stained and flaking. A king-sized bed with an ornate, wooden banister took up most of the room. The small area consisted of an end table and a dark brown dresser. A naked bulb hung from a black cable that dangled out of the yellow ceiling.

Sitting on the bed was a young Mexican with a shaved head and the standard cholo uniform of a white tank top and khakis. This was Abel. On the dresser was an open compact mirror with three lines of crystal displayed across it.

Abel stood up, "Heard Rodolfo outside, *guero* - don't worry 'bout him. That tweeker's just the watchdog, *no mas.*"

I croaked yeah or it's okay or some stupid comment.

Abel stepped over to the dresser and fingered the compact mirror. "Mario told me you wanna buy some crystal? How much?"

"A dime," I said.

Abel paused, glanced at Mario, then me.

"Is that it?" Abel asked.

"For now, yeah," I said. "I need to know if this shit is any good or not."

The young cholo went into his pusher spiel, "Well, I don't have to explain to you, this is some good shit - best shit yer gonna find anywheres. I don't sell it to just anyone, you know. Only amigos. Since you are amigos with Mario, I can cut you a good deal." He pulled out a twenty peso note from his pants pocket and rolled it into a tube - pointing it at me. "You wanna try some?"

"I'd be happy to." I said with the blank look of a corpse.

I took the rolled note and stepped to the dresser. The tiny crystals were shiny and pure and resembled ground glass. I placed one end of the note to my nostril and vacuumed up a line. Habitually throwing my head back, I snorted down the residue. Within seconds, that tingly feeling shot up through my upper spine. I handed the note back to Abel.

"Nah." He casually protested, palms out. "Let Mario go next."

As Mario snuffed, Abel smiled at me, "Some good shit, huh?"

"Not bad," I said.

"Not bad!" Abel laughed psychopathological laughter. "Not bad, your friend says, Mario. *Payaso!*"

Mario passed me the rolled note and grunted, "I told you this was good."

Abel continued, "My homie Mario gets all his shit from me." He reached into his pants pocket, pulled out a dime bag, and handed it to me. I slapped a hundred peso note into his hand.

Abel smiled his con smile, spoke to me slow and sweet, like I was a retard, "Right...right. Now, I need you only to buy from me, got it? If you need any more just get a hold of Mario and he'll bring you over here. Don't come by yourself. These pendejos who live on my street will kill your white ass."

I finished the line, wiped the residue on the compact mirror with my finger, and brushed it into my gums, "Hell yeah. Not too shabby. You got yourself a new client, man."

Mario moved towards the door, "We done? Yeah? *Orale.* Let's go."

Mario and I both said *laters* and walked through the other room to the exit. Esperanza pleasantly bid farewell to Mario - didn't say shit to me. Outside, the asshole on the second floor glared silently as we left.

"Okay, *mi amigo*," Mario warned. "Keep your eyes peeled for cops when we leave."

Mario decided he wanted some tacos and then some coke. and in that order.

Through sun-dappled, cobblestone streets of the Old Market, we bypassed fat and nasty whores who stood and waited forever, sucking on discolored, silvery teeth.

Shadowy phantoms lurked in alleys between closed shops enveloped by the reek of stale urine and vomit. Boarded doorways and crumbling masonry sheltered furtive and quivering junkies.

At a curb stall, we stopped for chicken tacos - slop on a plate - and downed two glass-bottled sodas. Ignoring dubious glances of wary pimps, we dodged chugging buses belching air so dirty it clogged your pores.

Mario and I made our way over to Coahuila Alley and up to Burrito Row. So named after the row of unwholesome burrito booths lined one after another on a side street.

Twenty-one-year-old Beto was working a stall – he smiled and greeted us as we approached. Beto possessed the type of classical good looks that old fags would write epic poems about.

Mario and I sat on wooden stools and made small chit-chat. The two immediately began discussing a serious matter. Beto gesticulated pleadingly at something Mario had said.

I ignored both of them as three doormen of the titty bar across the street – *The Mambo*

Room - caught glimpse of my gringo butt and began their hustle:

"Hey, buddy - no cover!"

"Over here! Big pussy!"

"Nice lady! Nice lady! Pussy women!"

I waved them away with a poker face, cause I had other business. They left sulking, only to pounce on four other American assholes.

The heated conversation between Beto and Mario *en Español* ensued and climaxed with Mario handing Beto some crumpled pesos. Beto contemptuously placed the notes under the till. A small, white packet of wax paper was slapped in Mario's hand and we walked away from the stall.

I nodded, *"Gracias!"*

"Orale." Said back. Beto didn't look up and continued to chop wilting vegetables.

"What's up with Beto?" I asked with obvious concern in my voice as we zig-zagged through bustling pedestrians.

"Nada." Was Mario's curt answer. He gave me a smirking, side glance, *"Nada* as in he only likes women, *guero."*

"Right. This is Tijuana." I informed jokingly as I lit a cigarette. "You know the right amount of money buys anything here. Or anybody." My last remark was coyly directed at Mario.

"Hey, now, watch it." Mario retorted in macho amusement. "I do it 'cause I like it."

"Sure, Mario, sure." I swung my arm over his shoulder as we continued down the busy sidewalk.

Mario casually removed the cigarette from my mouth and took a drag as we cut across Revolucion Avenue. We marched up the sidewalk passing loud and drunk *turistas*, passing taxi drivers on the hustle under glaring, ugly banners of teeny bopper discos which catered to the howling San Diego University crowd.

In front of a colorful cantina bloated with visiting American families, I briefly caught the eye of a famished zonkey and felt empathy for its sad existence.

Down a dead-end street paved in beer bottle caps to *Hotel Bombin* - Mario's rented room, a 100 peso a night trap. Mario paid the haggish lady behind a grill. I followed my friend up a white-tiled stairwell. He unlocked the deadbolt to one of the rooms in the dark hall and we entered.

He grabbed a strip of aluminum foil and folded a crease down the middle. Mario then pinched a few small rocks out of the Chinese rice paper and sprinkled the crystal substance onto the crease.

With sweaty, brown hands trembling as if it were his last, Mario lit the bottom of the foil strip with a lighter. He expertly rigged a straw from an empty ink pen tube.

In a graceless motion, the tube was placed in his mouth. His lips grimaced downward, eyes intent, Mario melted the small crystalline rocks into a liquid of Mercury-like substance.

The thick grey smoke with the smell of burnt metal funneled up into the pen and was deeply inhaled into charred lungs. He tilted the strip with care, letting the heavy metal fluid run down the course of the strip – greedily sucking at the fumes as he went. His face lit up like a pinball machine with esoteric results.

"*Orale.*" He finally exhaled and passed the strip to me.

I sat poised on the edge of a rickety, brown chair and followed his lead. The meth entered my lungs. Like a 240-volt circuit, the rush sped up my spine through the back brain and tingled my forehead. I lay back and listened down into myself.

Outside in the street of a late Mexican afternoon, cars honked and kids shouted in play. The avocado-painted room in which we sat was sparsely furnished - the smell of dust, soiled socks, and dried semen. Porno magazines – both straight and gay – lay strewn about. Many lewd and faded photographs were taped to the wall above the head of the bed.

I exhaled and wondered how much of this shit we had done. Tongue clicked against grinding teeth inside a mouth which tasted of aluminum. I was covered in a fine film of sweat. My eyes bounced around like the Cookie Monster. My seemingly elongated fingers twitched and twiddled uncontrollably as I passed the strip to Mario.

He sat across from me. Black, straight hair hung limply over savage, amber eyes. His toned, copper frame was shirtless from the heat. He removed it as soon as he entered the room, flinging it with masculine grace onto a pile of soiled clothes piled in a corner.

At that moment, I found him incredibly attractive. For a split second, I fantasized about what it would be like in a romantic relationship with him. I quickly pushed that unobtainable horror out of my mind.

"He cuts it himself." Mario finally said and, yes, Abel did a good job.

The piece which I had scored was a good size and got it half price. I knew the deal. Get me hooked and I will be a loyal customer.

It's working, I smiled to myself.

The worst porn in the world flickered on a small television set as Mario rocked back and forth, eyes dilated and red. He sat transfixed on the outdated imagery of a comically coifed skank getting pounded in the butt by an equally gelled and blow-dried stud.

I blearily glanced out the window. A brilliant, blue sky cascaded down on a dusty city.

Graffiti-covered buildings slowly crumbled into garbage, cars screamed, and ranchero tunes blared all in crystal clear focus. We both sat there in silence save for the *wackawacka wairn nairn* music from the 80s porn. Mario frustratedly slid a thin hand down his ravaged face.

We did another hit. Then another. And, then some more.

Mario phased out into Tweekerland and I lay down. Hyperventilating on the bed, I heard fucking phantom sounds (The sounds of fucking, you understand) inside the walls. I always do.

Take all this dick, bitch! The bed against the opposite wall - *thumpthumpthumpthump*. My teeth ground and my tongue clicked as I twitched like a short-circuited robot on the bed. My clothes clung to my wet body like a used condom.

I thought, *So this is what it has come to.*

Night fell as we lay side by side and shared a joint. Mario took it from his mouth and placed it between my lips. Not a single word was uttered during all that time as we both were consumed in mutual, and lonesome, addiction.

Hours passed as a mariachi band wailed ghostlike down a dark street. I stared catatonic up at the ceiling fan which whirled slowly - 5:20am. Mario silently snoozed next to me. The alarm went off.

There is nothing better - nothing in the world - than waking up in the warm arms of a handsome man on a chilly morning. Mario turned up at me, slow and sleepy like a turtle

- *buenas dias* - smiling, I gently rub the sleep out of his eyes with my thumb.

Together, we hit the shower with the tiles still cold and the full moon bright; stars twinkling. Downed a cup of instant coffee and out the door. We parted ways on a corner littered with trash as a mangy dog nuzzled through yesterday's garbage - it died a day later from contaminated, rotten meat.

I walked briskly, huddled in my black jacket with cigarette hanging and puffing through adobe and brick haciendas.

Fat, young whores - purposeful carriers of diseases - lurk in shadowy doorways selling their wares. Dirty latex stretched over bruises and pimples.

Tsk...tsk...wanna fuck me, baby.

I walked on, ignoring the filthy bitches.

The sun vibrantly peeked over the horizon and painted the city a lurid orange as pigeons flocked high above the green gymnasium where Mario and I had witnessed a midget *Lucha Libre* the week before. Funniest shit I ever sat still for.

Walking through Zona Norte that early with a fully charged tweek going on, I witnessed everything in focus - sharp and clear as if after a spring rain. I jolted into a café and ordered a cup of coffee and *pan tostada*.

In my pocket was the baggie, practically full. I sat and smiled inward while sipping my coffee in the assurance I would devour the entire contents of said baggie before heading back to work that evening.

15

I lay consumed in paranoid agitation. I hadn't slept for days. How many had it been? Nine? Ten? I lost track. As I was saying, I lay in my bed naked - sweating, twitching - sheets rumpled and filthy. It was unbearable. Enduring that insidious suffering alone.

Although the dark drapes were closed, the sun cut through random breaks of fabric like blinding blades of fire. The meth which I had acquired was gone and I hadn't any money to purchase more. Not for two days anyway. I didn't have to work the next couple of nights and I was utterly broke. I squirmed in aggravated convulsions.

Clunk! Clunk! Clunk!

What the fuck? Someone's outside!? I wasn't expecting anyone. Who could it be? Mooching friends? Cops? A random weirdo?

I bolted toward the window. I was certain about hearing someone out there. Peeking through musty drapes, the outside glare seared my retina as I scanned hastily for any person who would be creeping up the metal steps. No one.

I faltered and stood frozen in paranoid anticipation. That was when I heard them. The neighbors were having sex in an adjacent apartment. I lept onto the bed and crouched at the head of the mattress with my ear planted against the cold and concrete wall.

Thumpthumpthump.

It was muted and distant – but, I knew they were there!

I grabbed my pipe from the nightstand drawer. Sadly glancing at it, I woefully noticed the nearly depleted silvery film of residue lining the inside. I snatched my lighter and desperately smoked what was left.

Trembling, I rotated the pipe left and right skillfully not missing a spot - inhaling the acrid fumes - the taste of nickel in my mouth - twisting, turning the pipe. When all was completely gone and the bulb end was scorched and streaked with black char, I flipped the pipe around and carefully attempted to place the tiny opening of the bulb in my mouth and smoke what was left in the stem. I seared my lips in the process.

I yelped in pain and cursed myself as I impatiently waited the agonizing seconds for the bulb to cool. My fingers were now blackened from the carbon, shiny over the grime. I smoked what was left in the stem and lay propped up against the wall on sweat stained pillows.

With fucked up eyes, I glanced over toward the black-lacquer end table and discovered precious remnants of meth bits sprinkled amid the dust. I grabbed a plastic credit card which I used to line my dope up and carefully raked the debris over the top of the end table. With a degree of satisfaction, I accumulated a thin pitiful of crystal, dust, hair, and God knows what else.

I placed the scrapings into the pipe and lit up – listening to the popping of what wasn't meth and yet inhaled all the noxious fumes it emitted.

Thumpthumpthump. Fuck yeah! Oh, fuck me, baby! Like that! Yes!

I lay scrunched down against the wall with my ear attentive. Almost inaudibly, I sat and listened to the muted sounds of a woman moaning.

It was coming from the apartment on the opposite side of my living room!

I lept out of bed and dashed to the other room. I quickly dragged the futon couch from against the wall to the middle of the room. I yanked the mattress off the futon off the frame and placed it on the floor against the wall. Racing to the bedroom, I grabbed a pillow from the bed.

I returned to the living room and flopped onto the futon mattress. Ear firmly planted against the wall, I heard the muffled squeaking of bedsprings and the gasps and moans of sexual passion. I lay for an hour; listening to that distant, almost inaudible, groaning. My mind raced with lewd images of random, broken lust. Sweating and quivering, I began masturbating like an idiot - using the sweat of my palms as a lubricant. I must have laid there jerking off for hours.

Satiating myself, I licked dry, metallic-tasting lips and pressed my ear back against the wall. It was completely quiet - nothing but the reverberating echo of passing cars on the street below. I placed my trembling hand to my clammy forehead and hoarsely chuckled.

You, idiot! I thought. *There's no apartment on the other side of that wall. There's nothing there!*

It was becoming dusk and the room was quiet. Long shadows of late afternoon stretched across the bare walls. I rolled over onto my other side and lay staring at the dark, red carpet. To my horror, it was undulating in rapid movement.

Creeping slowly off the mattress on hands and knees – my sweat-dripping face inches from the funky-smelling carpet - I noticed ants crawling around mixed in with the black specks of the woven fabric.

At first, I caught the glimpse of only one. Then, from out of my peripheral vision, a few. Then the sheen of millions of black ants skittering about in a crazed frenzy.

I jolted up on my knees in confused horror. I blinked the sweat from my tired eyes. Shook my head. Slowly, like fog dissipating on a sunny morning from a chilled night, the insects faded away.

I stood up - wobbling from lack of food and sleep - and returned to my bed with a sore ear. My body was gummy and felt like rubber. The tweek was ebbing down and I knew I had nothing - no money, no articles to sell – nothing for the next two days.

I lay in my bed. My body was cold and shivered from dried perspiration. Long, silent moments passed. Finally, after days and nights, hypnotized by the immobile ceiling fan, I drifted into a dark and tormented sleep.

16

Cold and around 3am. I stood at the window of my room and gazed out into the silence of the sleeping neighborhood. From my second-story vantage point, I could hear the sighing of lonely taxis cruising for prey. The blanket of yellow streetlights stretched off into an obscure horizon. A white moon hung in a starless sky.

I took a long drag from my cigarette and pulled the dingy bathrobe closer to my body. I hated nights like this – long hours wallowing in fits of insomnia. It was insufferably quiet. I glanced down into a vacant, rubbly lot across from my apartment building. I wouldn't have noticed him if he hadn't moved.

He lurked in the shadows on a tattered, Mexican blanket – scuffed sneakers crossed, hands clasped at his chest as if lying in state. He reached over to a green, plastic bottle and took a swig of whatever liquid was inside. Long moments passed as I watched him. I watched - slowly smoking.

Calmly, he rose to his feet, slightly stretching. His broad shoulders shivered off the chill of the night.

I know how you feel, I smiled inward and from experience, *that concrete can get mighty cold.*

He was tall and lanky with long, black hair in waves which was tied back into a ponytail. His rugged, masculine face sported the obligatory goatee. The red-checkered shirt and blue jeans were old and well-worn. Dark skin soaked in the shadows.

He must be from the south, waiting to cross the border into the States. I was certain there were countless immigrants across Tijuana doing the same thing on this hopeless night.

He slowly meandered in and out of the grey shadows of the crumbling, red-brick walls which encircled the vacant space. He stopped, and then as I continued to watch, he crept slowly over to the first-floor window of another house which faced the lot.

Fingertips placed on the stucco wall, he stealthily moved up to the window and peered in. His black shadow extended, stretching and reaching the window before he did. He stood there – fixed on something within the house. I watched and slowly took another drag.

Quickly, he ducked down - paused – and as moments passed, cautiously peered back into the pitch-black window.

He turned and slinked back to his camp. He casually took another gulp of whatever was in the green, plastic bottle. Fishing for something in a bulging backpack, he placed the found object in his mouth, cupping it with the opposite hand to hide the flame of a lighter. He then took an enthusiastic inhale from the obvious glass stem. Tossing his head back, he blew great plumes of smoke up into the air. Returning the pipe and lighter to his bag, he furtively crept back to the window and peered in.

Moments passed. He tip-toed over to a part of the crumbling brick wall which rose a meter high and straddled it like a horse. He sat contemplating on the black pane a few feet away. Transfixed on the window, he then unbuttoned his dirty jeans and, in the half-light, pulled out an erection. Slowly he caressed it; in shadowy silhouette, his fingers slid the foreskin around the head. Even from my high vantage point, I could make out the moist sheen of the exposed tip. He silently lifted himself off of the wall and, with his erection swinging out in front of him, returned to the window. What did he see? A couple sleeping? A couple fucking? A small child snoring safely in their room? What was he looking at? I took another drag as he slipped up to the edge of the window and peered in, one hand on the sill, the other messaging his cock.

Sirens wailed and dogs barked as three police patrol cars careened down the street and hurtled passed - red and blue lights exploded across the lot. He quickly ducked from the window and scampered over to his camp. In one swoop; he collected his little plastic bottle, the backpack, and blanket, and escaped into the shadows of the night.

17

"Why do we always do this shit at night?" He grinned as he reached for the charred lightbulb with one hand and the flecked remnants of methamphetamine with the other.

I simply shrugged. What could I say? Philosophically, he was right. Why do we always do this shit at night? It's not as if we sleep during the day.

I glanced out the window. The moon swung round at supersonic speed. Up in the hills, a fat man echoed out in the distance, *"Tamales! Tamales!"*

Jose Perez placed his lighter under the lightbulb and with the opened copper end to his mouth - *flick!* Grey, swirling smoke of Blank Death warped around inside like a Texas tornado.

I saw the dope hit and his eyes lit up like fluorescent lamps. I took the bulb and repeated his actions. The metallic taste flowed down into my lungs, activating junk-hungry cells. The sensation of an electric current tingled up my spine, along the back of the skull, causing the hair to stand and pow! A magnificent rush to the forehead. I began to jerk in mechanical movements - vibrating like a tuning fork. My tongue writhed against grinding teeth.

Jose was lying back on the tattered futon dressed in a blue basketball tank-top with matching shorts.

My lascivious eye wandered across his limp, yet lengthy, cock resting on sagging balls. At any rate, that was how I fantasized it in my reeling mind. The flimsy material of the shorts accented his magnificent crotch in minute detail. I contemplated the phantom desire to reach over and grope that long fucker.

Unfortunately, my Adonis being helplessly, hopelessly heterosexual, I would not dare. I completely realized the handsome jerk was only here for my dope. At least he was good for casual conversation.

"You hear about Ivan?" Jose spat small balls of white spittle which flung through the air.

Clik-clik went his movements. A spastic robot. "Cops raided his place. Took everything."

"Really?" I croaked.

I didn't give a fuck - my thoughts wandered onto last night.

After an evening at a straight club with Jose, he picked up a chunky, American girl and we three drunkenly returned to my sordid flat. She wasn't ugly - big boobs, big hips - the kind of voluptuous torso straight guys jack off to. On the other hand, maybe it was just an easy lay.

Feigning sleep, I repaired to my room only to peer through the cracked door. What I witnessed in the blue light of the flickering television set was Jose screwing that cunt.

I didn't give a rat's ass about the girl; my bloodshot eye held its lustful gaze on Jose's long penis rapidly sliding in and out of her moist hole. On how hypnotically his balls slapped against her vaginal lips. A loveless love-making which terminated in a masculine grunt by Jose uttered only after performing five minutes of intoxicated, coital lunging. I anxiously ogled as he pulled out and a stream of white semen dribbled from the girl's cunt, and onto the futon's mattress. I lay down on my bed and took care of myself - falling asleep in that mess.

The next morning, both were gone. That macho fucker eventually returned in the afternoon and we went to score.

Jose and I stood in an alleyway of garbage and shit under a blinding yellow sun and dazzling blue Mexican sky. The watchful eye of a bitter taco vendor on the corner scrutinized our every move. My friend's paranoia mounted as a white sedan with darkened windows rolled up.

"Cartel" Jose muttered, hands in pockets, looking down.

After copping from a pusher known as Thing, broken sidewalks rushed under our feet back to my joint for a blast.

Nothing on television, only orange juice in the rattling fridge, a filthy bathroom overrun with ants. My carpet was covered in marijuana stems, food containers, meth papers - it's amazing what you noticed when you were tweeking.

Jose wanted to watch porn.

Fine, I thought, *torture me.*

As the video progressed, he achieved half a hard-on. Nothing is sexier than watching a cock grow in shorts unaided by hand. Inching upward, pulsing once, inching outward...

I digress.

In the most wicked and sleazy way, I leered at him and asked, "Hey, Jose, you wanna blow job?"

"Dude, you know I'm no *joto*." He retorted, all the while groping his semi-stiff organ. "You're cool and all, *guero*, but don't fucking ask me again."

I sank deep into the futon mired in angst and frustrated embarrassment. I wanted to be anywhere but in that room with him. I came to the despairing conclusion I was extremely attracted to Jose and like many homosexuals, it upset me not to possess the object in which I strongly desired. Why am I such a fool for these types of boys? Why am I addicted to this chaos and not only that, lustfully revel in it?

I hated myself. Inwardly mortified by my addiction and sordid homosexuality. So jaded had I become and antisocial. I loathe most faggots to this day. I see through all their amateurish attempts at deceit and seduction. I should know, I've tried them all.

I casually grabbed the lightbulb from off the end table - *flick!whoosh!* I glanced over at his long and lean body. I silently scrutinized those delicious, hazel-colored eyes encircled by thick, dark lashes, copper skin, short and shaggy ebon hair. His flared nostrils on a small, but hooked, Aztec nose. I lay there broken and in pain - vibrating in insidious lust amplified by the methamphetamine.

"That girl I met last night?" He finally said, white tongue licking thick lips. "I got a date with her again tonight. We supposed to meet outside *Las Pulgas*."

Las Pulgas was a straight dance club on Avenida Revo. Been there once. I had groped drunken boys as they passed with their girlfriends in the gyrating crowd. Always the classy one, me.

"So, I gotta jet. Gonna go home and get ready."

After liberally partaking in two more hits of my dope, Jose made his way to the door. We shook hands and mumbled 'see ya' to one another. I watched his skinny frame walk out, heard his feet clang down the stairs.

Two days later, Jose was found shot to death behind Hotel Coliseo off Avenida Coahuila. When I found out by another simpering and over-dramatic queen, I didn't care. I simply bought more dope and went on living.

18

I was fiending for a bump by the time my shift begun. Mario was nowhere to be found. However, there was one regular named Jerome - a young, black guy who sometimes helped me clean up the joint and received a whole day free in the theater. His deal was he never bought his speed. He would suck cock in lieu of free dope. Yet, once in a while, Jerome would accumulate a personal stash from an all-day marathon. I was anxiously hoping it to be one of those days.

At long last, Jerome made his way to the concession window. He noticed the decrepit state I was in. When our eyes met, I glared at him with pleading addiction.

"You holding, Jerome?" I croaked. "Tell me you got something."

"Naw, buddy." His attractive face frowned. "The place is dry tonight. I can't score neither."

I simply groaned as I gazed out the window and into the abyss.

Jerome stood silently staring at the monitor and watched a Latino woman lap at a white man's nuts. I turned back towards him.

"I'll tell you what, Jerome, if you have any contacts and make a run for me - I'll let you stay in the morning. Help me clean up and you can keep whatever you find."

Grinning, Jerome stated, "Okay. I know this cat down in Imperial Beach. Let me use the phone and I'll score some good shit for you!"

"Make my night, man." I agreed as I gestured toward the office telephone.

He punched in the digits. Apprehensive moments passed as Jerome made a deal, uttering yeah every three seconds.

He handed the receiver to me, "He wanna talk to you."

I spoke into the phone, "Yeah?"

A tinny voice rasped in hyped-up speed, "Hey! What's up? My boy Jerry tell me ya wanna score? I got whatcha need, man – I got it and it's the best. Best you ever gonna get with this price. Best, man – *the best!* If you're not satisfied - I'll personally give you a free bump. Sound good to you? Sound good? Yeah? How much ya need?"

The voice on the phone and I negotiated. With the last of my money, I slapped a fifty in his hand and sent Jerome on his way.

Two hours later the stupid fucker returned with less than half a bag. I was pissed. I'd always told myself, as did every learned junky in the theater, to never - *never!* - cop any shit from people you do not know. You'll get burned. That evening, I made that stupid ass mistake.

"Where's the rest of my dope, Jerome?" I snarled.

"That's all he gave me." He sniveled with a little boy hurt look.

I held the bag up to him, and roared, "Does this look right? *Does it?!* Where's the other half?!"

"I'm telling you, man – that's all he gave me!" He repeated with his palms pressed against the glass.

I noticed the dilation in his pupils and snarled. "Get the fuck outta here! You are barred from this place, understand?! Permanently!"

For an entire hour, Jerome remained outside of the box office window in the silent night. He sobbed and pleaded to be readmitted. Not only did I not let Jerome into the theater, but I also snorted all that shit in one sitting in front of him. Eventually, he vanished into the night.

I had no idea what that crap I bought was cut with, but I was a fucking mess. As the night progressed, I dropped things on the floor, spilled coffee everywhere, and the worst part - the absolute insidious part - I began chicken pecking.

On every surface, throughout the office, there was a fine layer of debris. Asbestos, peeled paint chips, dirt, and dust bunny-coated shelves, wood beams, counters, and office equipment. I devoted the next five hours of my shift - with a flashlight in hand – meticulously combing over every inch of that office checking, scrutinizing, and probing every single, minute dust particle. I kind of remembered earlier I had dropped several specks of crystal somewhere - I was certain of it! And, God damn it - I was determined to find it!

Down on all fours behind the metal filing cabinet I had shifted out of the way, my flashlight swooshing back and forth, I picked up bits of asbestos and dust with trembling thumb and forefinger – shiny over the dirt. I held the particles up close to my glasses, wincing - then chucking it over my shoulder, continuing to the next, then the next, then the next.

There was a loud knock on the counter at the concession door. I popped up. It was Bruce - an ancient, pudgy fairy who was good friends with the manager of the theater.

I stood in front of him with eyes wide and dilated, cheeks withdrawn, dirty from the floor.

He inquired in a soothing voice, the kind of calm tone one uses when speaking with the insane, "What are you doing?"

"Nothing!" I spat. "I dropped something and I was looking for it. What's up? Whatta ya need? How can I help you?" The last three questions shot out as if one word.

Bruce raised a fey eyebrow, "Are you all right?"

"Yep! Never felt better! What can I get ya?!"

I was a sweating, galvanized mess.

He waited for a beat, then said, "Just a coke."

"You got it, Brucie!" I snatched the bills from his hand, darted over to the mini-fridge, and grabbed a soda. On my way back, I dropped the can and watched it roll into a corner. "Woah! Probably don't want that one!" I over-dramatically gesticulated as I spoke. "Open that fucker up and – *kerblooey!* – one helluva money shot!"

I burst into insane, uncontrolled cackling. He stared back with a face as blank as a poker dealers.

With condescending tones, Bruce ordered another coke, and returned silently into the theater.

19

As only a junky can understand another junky, an alcoholic can share solace with an alcoholic, and a queer can spot another fag in a room full of filthy breeders; could anyone understand the despair of insidious depression which wracked my trembling form for the past few days.

I had hit rock bottom. Nothing interested me. I did not go out. I did not socialize. If I attempted any form of social interaction, I simply glared at those garrulous beings in hate-filled, annoyed contempt. I did not write. I did not eat. I did not sleep. All things - *all of them* – which had previously given me any remembrance of joy; now simply awarded me with nothing but despair and emptiness.

Horrible depression. Wracked with it. Enveloped in it.

In my darkened apartment, I sat naked on my futon couch for hours and stared at nothing. Yet, my mind reeled with millions upon millions of nostalgic images.

Why was I in Tijuana? Why did I shift from a relatively comfortable existence – a decent job, a nice apartment, a circle of caring friends - only to wind up in a ratty slum with no furniture save for a smelly bed, filthy futon, and a television propped up on plastic milk crates? I rarely kept food in the kitchen on account I did not eat - the refrigerator never functioned properly anyway, keeping the ever-present carton of orange juice tepid at best.

When I first relocated to Tijuana, the apartment was full of new furniture purchased while I was employed as a front desk clerk at a respectable hotel in downtown San Diego. On account of my fledgling habit, that job was short-lived. In time, as my addiction grew, my possessions were sold or traded for dope. My bank account had been depleted and canceled a long time ago.

I sat with my body cold from the film of dried sweat which covered my withered torso. I held the charred glass pipe in my dirty hand, fingers coated in black carbon. A wave of utter sorrow and loss swept over me.

I lay down on my side and began to uncontrollably sob. Where did I go wrong? I had no one to blame but myself. I lost everything from friendships to personal possessions; degenerating into a self-absorbed, arrogant mess. And the company I kept - if I cared to keep - all junkies, thieves, male prostitutes, hustlers, con men, or back-stabbing faggots. I trusted not one of them and detested their companionship.

Yet, the loneliness howled through me like a black wind. Viciously stripping away in chunks whatever sociable, caring person I once was.

I reined in my deep sobs and concluded I desperately needed to take control of my situation. I had to stop. I had to find a way out of this nightmare I can't wake up from. I sat back up, took the empty baggie which lay on the wooden arm of the futon couch, and skillfully extracted the few, precious flecks of meth which remained. I dropped them carefully, lovingly, into the bulb of the pipe.

As I lit up, inhaling those grey fumes of grief and destruction, I told myself, *Tomorrow - tomorrow, I will quit.*

20

Wanna-be gangsters stood on a corner chewing on toothpicks and flicking switchblades. Baggy clothes of ghastly colors - almond, peach, florescent blue - fluttered in the tepid wind.

"You lookin'?" One jerked his head at me.

"No." I walked on under black, cold stares.

Trash-lined streets crawled with obscene prostitutes of both sexes - the women were especially nasty under the blue neon of a dark, crumbling adobe night. Banda music and hawkers of insidious filth beckoned to enter their traps. I clutched my wallet and moved on.

Squeezed past an armada of nasty whores brandishing silver-capped teeth and exposing their undulating udders as I made my way over to *Bar Kin-kle.*

I entered the hazy, smoky den and found the cantina crowded with Zona Norte's finest. I took a table occupied by an old vato who sat at a dented, metal table with white, plastic lawn chairs. He smiled and nodded at me. We say nothing to each other as a female midget skank obscenely danced in the middle of the room to *Jailhouse Rock* thumping from the jukebox.

I lit a cigarette and gazed around the bar.

Kin-kle was a long, low-ceilinged cantina with rusted, aluminum stools facing the counter. Opposite the weathered bar, a row of tables lined the wall. Boxes of beer were stacked against the back next to a rockola - that's a jukebox to the ignorant who don't speeky the Spanish.

Mario walked in, strung out on his own shit, and plopped next to me a greasy, giggling mess. I said howdy, he said hi. He ordered a caguama after procuring one of my cigarettes.

"How's the book coming along?" He asked.

"Fine." I took a swig from my caguama bottle, savoring that cold, charcoal taste that filtered down my pipes. "I'm calling it *Speed Queen.*"

Mario rolled his eyes over at me as he blew cigarette smoke up to the rotted rafters, "You would. Speaking of..."

He stood up and walked into the mensroom. A stale tang of beer, piss, and shit mixed with odorous bleach wafted through the entrance and saturated the cantina.

I waited a cigarette and Mario returned.

"Hurry up", he said. "I left something in there for you."

I made my way into the toilet.

A squat Indian stood in a corner holding the unsightliest mop in the world. He motioned to the metal-encased stall. "Go in, *guero* - it's for you."

I entered and waiting on the empty toilet paper dispenser were three lines of that sweet, white powdery stuff.

God bless you, Mario.

Mechanically, I whipped out a peso note; rolled it into a cylinder, bent over, and *snortsnortsnort!* I jolted up, snuffing and hawking. *Pop! Crackle! Pow!* I staggered out of the stall, a curt, two-fingered Boy Scout salute to mop guy, and returned to the table.

I plopped into my seat and Mario took another cigarette.

I gazed at him with sparkly eyes and smiled, "You're so good to me."

He smirked downward, "I know."

An inebriated Indian sat across from us, swaggering and leaning in his seat. His eyes were unfocused and he dribbled saliva from an open mouth.

He lifted two fingers to his lips and asked with a thick accent "One cigarette?"

I smiled and handed him one. He was tall with an athletic build. He wore a red t-shirt, blue jeans with woven sandals.

I asked in Spanish, "You wanna beer?"

He nodded. I ordered another plastic cup. When the waiter left after serving us, we three *salud* each other from a fresh caguama bottle. The old vato who sat at our table stared vacantly out into space.

Like an atomic blast, the overpowering reek of stainky, unwashed pussy assaulted my nostrils.

I glanced in the direction of the offending odor and standing there was a short hag with a demented smile plastered on an ancient face. She wore a filthy, rose-patterned smock over dingy capris. Her feet blackened from the absence of footwear. The auburn hair was matted on a prunish head from grease and grime. I'd seen her about, living in the streets, rummaging through trash bins for scraps of food.

She stood smiling. "Meester, one cigarette?"

Jesus, I thought, *Who the fuck am I? The Borrachos Benevolence Society?*

I gave her one, anyway. With that, she proceeded to plop next to our new and plastered hottie and without exchanging one word, they went at it like two overheated hogs, kissing and sucking each other's lips loudly. Mario and I looked on in absolute disgust as the handsome drunk's tongue devoured her rancid, toothless hole.

"Mario, let's get out of here." I sighed.

"I agree." He mumbled.

Outside, Mario and I stood under an awning as the rain began to come down in yet another hopeless attempt to wash away the filth of The City.

Indians and cholos and terrified tourists dashed past us in the wet night. We stood in that neon labyrinth, speechless, feeling the dope, and taking turns smoking my last cigarette. Mario and I popped and jerked in stylized, mechanical movements as the meth began to take its full effect.

A cigarette between us goes by and Mario placed a thin hand on my back. "*Guero*, let's get a room."

"Yeah?" I said with a raised eyebrow.

"Yeah." He repeated, giving me that look of longing.

I smiled to myself. I'd seen that look before on horny dogs. My stomach knotted in anticipation.

I followed my Dark Knight as we jumped over incandescent pools and dodged kamikaze taxis to Hotel Coliseo. I plunked down the pesos to the stinkbomb who sat behind the grate and we shot up the old, wooden stairs to the third floor. The dank hallway smelt of mildew and stale feces.

The rented room consisted of only a mattress on the floor and an antique brown dresser. I took a piss in the dingy, white-tiled bathroom and returned to find Mario shivering naked under a thin, pink blanket.

The musty room was muted in long, dark shadows as I undressed and lay next to him.

Silently, hands stroked over bodies, tongues probed, organs stiffened. I'll never tire of Mario - always up for kicks. Our passion peaked as Mario placed my feet up on his shoulders, spat into his palm, and glided his long penis into me. Thrusting and lunging until eventually he yanked out and splattered his semen onto my heaving chest. We fell into next to each other, the meth vibing on supersonic frequencies through our lust-filled minds. After our breathing subsided, we did it again.

Just before dawn, we both stood outside in the enveloping fog. Mario hit me up for 100 pesos before I hailed a cab back to my trap. He slid a small paper folded in a square into my palm as we shook hands goodnight.

Slouched in the back seat, I smiled inward as the taxi pulled away - Mario always knew how to make a drab night delightful.

21

The sun slowly crawled over the horizon. Off in the mist, a dog barked - a car passed. The depression was hitting me in full force. I had been up for days now and my mind felt like mayonnaise.

The apartment – or what was left of it - was a filthy, dank den which smelled of burnt metal and musty clothes. The mattress was exposed from messed sheets - stained in sweat, semen, and God knows what else. Without all the furniture I used to have, the room was empty with the long shadows of a prison.

I lay on my bed with a cigarette in hand and stared at the spotted ceiling. I felt nothing. I had nothing. *Nothing.* I was so alone. I could not, would not, fall in love with anyone. Then again, on my end, what was left to fall in love with? Every relationship I attempted since my move to Tijuana incessantly terminated in psychotic fights usually instigated by my own sick mind.

The loneliness draped over me like a cold, black shroud. My mind spun assisted by the few dozen hits which I indulged in throughout the night.

What is wrong with me? I thought.

I began contemplating every alternate route my life could have taken - remaining in Los Angeles, holding a decent job, becoming a writer, or even making movies. All those nostalgic plans collapsed into failure.

Everything I had attempted ran into ruin.

I never once received any moral support from a vile and vindictive family, never any trusting friendship from money-obsessed, conning acquaintances, and I won't even go into an explanation of the dope addicts I associated with. Their sole concern focused on attaining drugs. Whatever amount they did obtain, it was never enough (like me, it was never enough - *ever*) So, they would go after my meager supply similar to a shark stalking a wounded sea creature.

I lay there and simply wanted to sink deeper into the mattress. I strained to focus on the future.

One time, long ago, I encompassed lofty plans. Living in a posh house in the Hollywood Hills with a handsome, young lover, famous on behalf of my literary achievements, attending upscale parties, television spots on celebrity talk shows, getting written up in the papers - all which faded into a choking mist.

I had no future.

Over the years, I had acquired a mental state of such downward bleakness that whenever I did think of that hopeful future, I was instead met with a dark, cold abyss in my mind's eye.

The depression absolutely consumed me with those whirling memories. I never felt as sad, alone, and hopeless as I did at that moment. What was the point of going on when there was no point? I should simply die. It struck me as quite logical. Who would miss me? I would miss no one. I wouldn't have to worry about jobs, rent, or my shit being stolen by those damn naco junkies.

My already drug-ravaged face wrinkled into worry and sadness. I looked over at my end table - scorch marks, candy wrappers, cigarette butts, and empty meth bags were strewn across it.

I picked up my only meth pipe and held it between my thumb and forefinger. I examined its charred glass sides – sparkling white residue in streaks along the shaft behind black char. My rage erupted like a mushroom cloud. It was this shit's fault. Every calamity and misfortune was the curse of this fucking addiction I had acquired.

In a flaring fit of anger, I forcefully flung the pipe across the room and shattered it against the white-washed concrete wall.

I yelped and lept out of bed toward the shards lying on the dirty carpet. I picked up the glass chunks, cradling those precious pieces. *What have I done? Oh jeez!* I looked at the pieces and felt an emotional pity for the broken parts. I felt a saddened, kindred spirit to the little fucker, and I just killed it!

I squat there on my haunches. Feeling so sad, so invariably sad. Especially toward the stupidity of the situation. Utter despair coursed over me. There was nothing. I had nothing.

Nothing.

Acting on impulse, I rose, went into the kitchen, and retrieved a butcher knife from the cupboard drawer. I knew what I wanted to do. Why not? What reason was there for me to continue like this? None. Who would care if I was still around? No one. My friends would have forgotten me in a week. Nothing. My parents did not give a shit, so why should I? Nothing, nothing, nothing...

I stood grasping the knife, clutching it in my right hand. I balled my left fist and raised my left arm. The steel felt cold against my skin as I executed that first slice. A trickle of blood formed and streamed a thin line down to the elbow.

I was struck with sobering terror. *What the fuck was I doing?!* I threw the knife into the sink and snatched a rag off a hook to stop the bleeding. The tingling pain began to throb. I was embarrassed. Completely mortified by the foolish attempt I committed.

I hurried into the bathroom and grabbed a wet towel. I examined the wound. It seemed I didn't cut that deep.

Grasping the blood-soaked towel around the wound, I walked to a corner *farmacia* and bought a roll of bandages and a bottle of iodine from an unconcerned clerk.

I returned home and dressed my arm the best I could. When done, I glimpsed in the mirror at the ravaged visage which stared back. Such a countenance of hatred lined the sallow face. The darkness under glassy eyes. The perpetual grimace. I sighed and accepted my fate. A life of endless sorrow and misery.

I need to get out...get away, was the only thought which burned in my mind.

Shortly afterward, I found myself sitting in a nearby park. Children played, vendors sold balloons and flavored ice, couples strolled lost in love. A pleasant breeze rustled through vibrant trees under a sky a bright, cloudless blue. Around me pulsed the beat of life.

I sat on the concrete bench like a disgusting stain on an idyllic painting - a vulgar mark on the world. Such a depression.

I held my head, cigarette dangling from my lips - what an utter loser I was. Such a disappointment. I have failed at so many attempts to better my life - hell, I even failed at ending it.

My focus settled on a youthful couple who lay in the grass under a shaded tree. The boy smiled; the girl bashfully laughed. They momentarily gazed into each other's eyes and fell into an emotional kiss.

I let out a desperate sigh and squished my cigarette out with the toe of my shoe. I stood up and walked over to Coahuila Avenue to buy more dope and purchase a new pipe.

22

I stumbled out of my apartment into the God awful bright sun. The color was drained from my face and replaced with the ever-attractive beads of constant sweat. The lifelessness within my eyes masked the headache which ripped through every thought.

Here was the nausea, the irritation, the itching, the biting and tearing at every little moment of every little minute of every little hour of every little day. The pain of the beast which struggled through its final death was greater, compared to the pain which brought it to life.

How many days had I been without sleep? I lost count. I broke from my self-induced recluse and, for some damned reason, walked downtown to a restaurant because I was fiending for a fruit salad. And nowhere else in Tijuana could anyone prepare a fruit salad as they did at *Café Norteño*.

As I was saying, I stumbled down Revo and over to Plaza Santa Cecilia. The café tables were full of expat boylovers and the hustlers who preyed on them. They sat as they always had, cooing and cackling, ripping one another to shreds with gay double entendre, pointing and giggling at every passing crotch. That image will be forever frozen in a flashbulb of stasis.

I flopped down in a chair at an empty table by the yellow-tiled wall as waiters dashed past at supersonic speeds. The café was a symphony of patter and clinking utensils integrated with the obligatory ranchero music blaring from the jukebox. I sat twitching and sweating; ignoring curious glares of disgust from the other patrons. I realized I must have looked like shit. I held no shame. No dignity left.

I slumped in my seat, hypnotized by the sounds of passing cars outside in the street. They seemed to whisper my name as they whooshed by.

I barely noticed when one of the waiters approached my table. It was Raphael, a handsome, young man built like a bulldog. I'd known him casually since I first arrived in Tijuana. Under the tattooed, tough physique, I found him to be a very gentle and soft-spoken person. He stood there a moment, giving me a curious look as I swayed catatonically back and forth.

Raphael wiped the plastic, red checkered tablecloth with a dirty rag, "What is wrong with you, *guero*?"

I jumped in my seat at his words, knocking silverware onto the floor. Perspiration poured off my face, my mouth was dry, and my teeth ground loudly as I reached down to quickly picked up the utensils.

"Nothing!" I spat. My eyes ping-ponged around the room. "Gimme a fruit salad, will ya? No papaya. Horribly allergic to papaya."

He leaned to one side, staring at me, "You are on something, I think."

With a paranoid start, I veered towards the door, certain shadowy phantoms were lurking - my mind spun in and out of focus. I then swung back in my seat and looked up at Raphael, "No - no, man. Just a little tired." I wiped the sweat off my forehead and rubbed my hands on dirty jeans, leaving a moist mark. "Holy fuck, it sure is hot today, huh?" I chuckled in a futile attempt to change the subject.

Raphael slowly shook his head in shame, "*Oye, vato,* you need to cut that shit out. You look horrible. Your face - it looks so sick."

I watched as he entered the kitchen to place the order. My mind began to reel concerning the loathing and humiliation of what I had become. I started to spiral deeper down into despair.

Someone sat at my table. I glanced up to see a rentboy who I knew named Diego. A doe-eyed waif of sixteen, Diego was a seasoned veteran at soliciting the old Americans who trolled the plaza. A dingy white t-shirt and dirty, blue jean shorts covered a scrawny, pale frame. His long and hairless legs were a mass of scabs and open sores.

"Mind if I sit with you?" He asked.

"Yeah. Sure. Why not." I mumbled.

Other rentboys - especially the ones who prowled the Plaza - never asked, they simply did. I recalled many a time how I would be sitting in a café and one of those obnoxious fuckers would brazenly plop down in front of me, not uttering a word, order something, and then expected me to pay.

More often than not, before I could make a protest, they would invite one of their sulking friends lurking nearby.

Inevitably, the smooth-talking and coy sexual innuendos would issue forth and attempt to dispel any discontent. It obviously worked on other unwise, sexually frustrated expats - however, I usually told them to beat it or I would simply stand up, pay my bill, and split.

I tolerated Diego; he was more or less genuinely courteous and exhibited a little respect.

He sat looking at me as I jerked and quivered opposite him.

"You look like you're having a good time." Diego finally said with a sarcastic grin. A series of small, puss filled boils formed on the lower edge of his supple, pouty lips.

Hanging my head, I blurted, "I can't live like this anymore. This city is killing me. If I don't find a way out and soon, they're going to find me dead in some fucking alley. I can't ask for help; all my friends have turned their backs on me. I hate my job – I'm going to lose that real quick anyways. But, where can I go? It's too goddamn expensive to live in San Diego. I'm at my wit's end...I honestly don't know what to do."

I glanced at him momentarily, slightly embarrassed by that uncontrolled barrage of blathering. In his questing eyes, I realized he understood completely the words of my desperate, disjointed rant.

As Raphael arrived and placed a soda on my table, Diego ordered a *fresca* and said, "In two weeks, I am going to Ciudad Juárez. Do you know where that is?"

I shook my head no.

"It's on the border, opposite of El Paso, Texas. I understand you like living in Mexico. Why don't you move to Juárez and get away from all this crazy life?"

Diego took a sip of his drink as his big, brown eyes scanned my distraught face. He continued, "I mean, what is there here for you? For myself, absolutely nothing. I am returning home to live with my mother. In Juárez at least, I can start over again and not do the things I have to do here to survive. You should go to Juárez and have a fresh start, *guero.*"

I deliberated the suggestion, weighed the outcome. I rubbed my raw nose with a dirty finger, shiny over the dirt, "Yeah...why not?"

Raphael served my order. He stood there glancing at Diego and then looked at me, "I used to live in El Paso. It is a small town - but nice. The change would do you good, I think."

For a few minutes, Diego and I sat there in complete silence. Yet, we shared the same thoughts. The contemptible hatred of our current state of affairs. I pensively picked at my salad - swirling the fork in the mess of honey and cottage cheese.

I nodded, looking up to meet Diego's gaze, "You know what, kid? You're right. I have absolutely nothing to lose. I'm going to do it. Tomorrow, after I get off work, I'm out of this fucked up shithole."

23

I walked with determination in the chilled, wet twilight through darkening streets of Tijuana. I was in Zona Norte to score for dope. Cold, dirty, depressing - this was the far north area of The City, beyond the neon arabesques of whore houses and discos. Shattered sidewalks and crumbling adobes faded into sordid, wooden shanties that resembled chicken shacks littered by piles of moldy rubbish.

I bypassed tattered dwarfs and filthy catatonic citizens with boneless flippers for arms. Silent specters with cleft lips and horrible skin diseases which resembled the end result of atomic radiation. No one smiled, no one spoke. People shuffled in silence; their faces wrapped in dingy, grey scarves against the night air.

I darted past the watchful taco vendor into a filthy alleyway strewn with garbage and dog feces. Little kids ran and played about as I made my way to a huge, blue windowless wall - two stories of solid concrete.

Down at street level was a hole about half a foot wide which had been chiseled into the wall. I furtively glanced to my left and right – noticing a Mexican who rummaged through a giant pile of trash against the opposite dusty building. He was emaciated and wore colorless rags for clothing. Our eyes met and that contact confirmed we both suffered the same addiction.

I reached into my pants pocket and pulled out a fifty peso note. I leaned toward the hole and blurted, *"Oye!"* (Hey!)

Momentarily, a huge, brown, hairy arm poked out of the hole and snatched up my money. I lit a cigarette and waited.

Down at the end of the alley, two cops patrolled on bicycles. The grease-stained taco vendor cut and chopped onions with a loud *clop-clop!* while he kept his eye fixed on me. A black, mangy dog lumbered down the dusty street covered in sores. The mongrel's eyes were caked in puss, tongue lolling out with saliva that splattered onto the pavement.

Psst! Psst!

The monstrous paw extended again from the cavity in the wall and dropped a small, square-folded, wax paper into my needy hand, and then disappeared into the hole's blackness.

"Thank you, Thing," I whispered and then hurriedly walked toward the corner.

Past the wall of grabbing hookers of both sexes smiling behind stained teeth, past the hawkers of lewd trinkets and self-indulgence, past the cholos inquiring if I 'needed anything', past the deformities and their questing, filthy hands outstretched forever – I made my way up to the corner of Calle Primero and Revo.

I stood at the base of the Millennium Arch admiring a panoramic view of The City - caressing the dope in my pocket, smoking a cigarette with the other hand.

Two paddy wagons hurtled by. The open beds of the white trucks held about five prisoners each as they careened past. The captives appeared forlorn and dirty and beat with heads hung down in shame or fatigue.

As the second cruiser shot by kicking up swirling plumes of dust, one of the prisoners in the back looked up and our eyes met. It was little Mario. His bottom lip was bloated and purple, eyes blackened, forehead caked with blood. When he saw me, he smiled.

"Guero!" He yelled out before he was too far away down the street to yell anything else. Those silver-capped teeth glared out from a ravaged face.

He saw me grin and curtly nod my head in acknowledgment. His battered face faded into the distance as the paddy wagon hastily continued to the police substation. I stood there a moment, the convoy lost far away in haze and traffic. Moments after the two wagons were well out of view, I contemplated in bitter sadness at the sight of Mario. Probably the only person in this nightmare I considered a friend. It was an inevitable omen. I turned and walked back to my apartment.

The entire way home, I kept rolling the words around in my head, *I have to stop...I have to stop this! I can't go out like that...*I told myself I was going to quit. Quit and leave Tijuana for good. Right after I finished the meth I had just scored.

24

It had been two weeks since the party. Two long weeks had passed when that fag, Ismael, remarked on how lost I looked. I came to the sordid conclusion. he was right.

Over the past five years during my stay in Tijuana, my addiction had devoured everything I held dear - friends, personal effects, my health. I hit the end of the road.

The main question was - what did I plan to do about it?

My emotions reeled in contempt as I hopped off the trolley in downtown San Diego and trudged to work. I stood outside the theater and finished a cigarette - my stomach was hurting. I felt as if I was going to vomit. I contemplated turning around and not coming back.

Putting the cigarette butt out with my foot, I entered the office ten minutes before my shift began.

Bill stood there chomping on garlic and stupidly glaring at me through his grimy, bottle-thick glasses. "Hey! There ya are, man! Oh boy, is Bob pissed at you. He says he's been getting shocking comments regarding you from the theater patrons. Says that you been treating them rudely. The regulars stopped coming and he's losing money."

I ignored him and silently began to count out the register. My head spun from the amount of garlic that wafted through the air.

"I wouldn't worry about it, though." He continued chewing. "Bob's just mad 'cause he can't control Keith and he's taking it out on us."

Us? I thought. *What's this us shit?*

I was certain it was an all-out effort to dump his frustrations on me and me alone.

Mercifully, Bill left right at the moment my shift began and didn't hang around as he usually did. It was a relief; I seriously did not think I could tolerate any more of his gossipy shit. My mind was heavy in contempt and hate for the place and everyone associated with it.

An hour passed and the phone rang. It was Bob.

He husked through heavy-labored breathing, "How's everything going?"

I knew this was going to be bad. He always began with the buttering up routine before he dropped the ax.

"Things are fine, Bob." I croaked flat, toneless, dead.

There was a dramatic pause before he released an onslaught of faggoty fury.

"Now listen to me, ya goddam motherfucker!" Bob blubbered rapidly.

I stared into nothing, zoning him out.

His attempt at abuse continued, "If you wish to remain in my employ, you had better

228

get your shit together. I am receiving far too many complaints concerning you."

Another long pause for dramatic effect. Somebody should give this motherfucker an Oscar.

"Are you listening to me? Do you understand what I am saying? What, you have nothing to say? *Ugh!* You are spineless, you know that? I should come down there right now and throw your ass out! You are lucky – damn fucking lucky - I have to wait for Keith to come home or I would be at my theater right now and toss your ass into the street. Are you listening? Are you there?"

I remained silent, seething with contempt.

"Say something if you want to keep your job, asshole!" He bleated with the firm assurance he was in total control.

"I'm here." I finally said.

"You act as if you don't even care what I'm saying to you."

Thank you for stating the obvious.

"You can be damned sure I will be there first thing in the morning, you worthless fuck, and when I arrive we will discuss in length this shitty, little attitude of yours! Got that!?"

229

He hung up before I could answer. I was livid. That was it - I made my decision. I ripped out a strip of aluminum foil and smoked the last of my dope. Anger and meth do not mix; any addict can tell you that.

As the night dragged on, I paced uncontrollably back and forth in the office. I resentfully admitted patrons at the box office and radiated waves of toxic hostility toward the ones who dared to bother me at the concession window. My mind spun in a vortex of self-loathing and anger.

"I have to stop, I have to stop!" Was all I kept muttering as I paced back and forth the length of the office with my fists clenched and trembling.

Nostalgia flashed before me, all the friends who were now dead or incarcerated, all the money which had been plundered and pissed away to support my addiction, all the crap which I had put myself through. The long nightmare had come to a vacuous end. I was done. *Done!*

At that moment I made the dream of leaving into a reality. There is nothing - *nothing* - better in the world than committing a crime and getting away with it. I looked at the open register till and the whirring video machines. I decided to pilfer what I could from the office – purely from spite - and leave for Texas as Diego had suggested.

It was the still of the night. I glanced up at the clock on the wall; it read 3:47am. In the theater, all was quiet except for the grunts and moans of the movie.

I casually walked over to the cash register and emptied it out. I took the bills and left the coins. It was an okay night and the count came to six hundred and fifty dollars. I knew if I was going to take this trip, I required all the money I could get hold of.

The movie in the theater ended, so I cued up the next feature on one of the two VCRs which were in the office. As for the one that wasn't being used, I decided to take it, too. I disconnected the machine and placed it onto the blue recliner.

However, I needed more! And, I knew exactly where.

On the opposite side of the entrance hall was a service door where inside lay the safe. When the building was converted into a theater, the contractors must've built that small room quickly. Though it was solid with wood panels and frame, it did not quite reach the high ceiling, leaving the top open. I knew, and Bob knew, over half the time the damn safe wasn't even locked. I stood in front of the cubicle's door and frowned inward, I didn't have the keys to the safe room, but that wasn't going to stop me.

Bad ideas are seldom boring.

I grabbed the folding chair which sat at the cinema's entrance and placed it next to the door. Hoisting myself up, I scampered over the wall - my stomach was scratched from the splintered wood frame, my shirt smeared in dust and old, flaking asbestos. I flipped myself over the top and landed hard on my feet inside the cubical.

There lay the safe - dusty and impregnable. That repulsive fucker Bill had locked it this time! *Fuck! Of all nights!* I checked the lever in the hope it was merely closed and not locked. It was shut tight.

Anxiety at the very act of what I was committing ran cold up my spine. I had to split quickly before one of Bob's nosey friends wandered up to the concession stand and notice I must "Be Up To Something" and warn Bob before I could get away.

I returned to the office, grabbed my jacket, snatched up the pilfered VCR, and headed out the door. I didn't even bother to lock up the box office.

As I darted out of the cinema and into uncertain liberation, crazy, meth-induced images ran through my mind.

Inwardly, I chuckled at the delusion of Bob arriving the following morning to an office stripped bare. The unmistakable evidence of fiending junk-food junkies who committed unspeakable sex acts in the concession area. The storage shelves ransacked by frustrated crackheads who grabbed handfuls of pornography to sell on the streets. Wild-eyed tweekers who disassembled every electronic component then tore the office to shreds in exasperation at the attempt to reassemble the equipment all over again.

It was petty revenge on my part. But, revenge of necessity.

My heart raced. I was tweeked out of my gourd as I strutted down the dark and misty morning street toward the nearest trolley station carrying a stolen VCR with wires dangling in my arms like entrails.

At the station, I ignored sniffs of disdain and loathsome glances from fellow commuters as we silently waited in the pre-dawn night. It was nearly 5am and the train had already begun running.

Realizing there were no patrols that early, I hadn't even bothered purchasing a ticket. I shifted my feet, averted my gaze, and waited - sweating and shaking.

I jumped on an arriving train. I sat and listened to the *clakclakclak* of the rails as we raced down toward the Mexican border, enveloped in the euphoria of what I had just committed and the thrill of what I was going to do.

I made a mad dash across the frontier and hailed a taxi. I didn't even consider walking to my apartment - not with me tweeking, clutching a stolen VCR, and a load of cash in my pocket.

I reached my place full of angst and apprehension. I tossed the VCR on the bed and acted fast. Grabbing my old duffel bag from the closet, I crammed what ratty clothes and few personal items I had into it.

The realization of what I was doing and why began to sink in and it stopped me in my tracks. I began to think about how I was a methamphetamine addict and what that entailed. A fucked up mess, that's what. I sat on the corner of the bed and glanced around the dark, musty room.

A kaleidoscope of fractured images swarmed in front of me concerning all the experiences and people in this mad, insane city in which I had gotten trapped. I thought of what life would be like in Ciudad Juárez? A better existence? Finally, attaining a loving soul mate? Or would I wind up in the same pitfalls as those I was running from? Hell, I only had a vague idea where Juárez was.

My mind inevitably wandered to Mario and all the sordid adventures we had scoring for dope, the crazed late-night drinking, and the wild experiences at the theater. I was hoping to at least see him one final time before I cut out of town. I wondered how he would fare in the months to come. Jail? Death?

I recalled an over-exaggerated, tweek-fueled rant Mario once went into when I asked his opinion of tweekers as we lay naked next to each other on a sagging bed in a dark hotel room. Crumpled strips of scorched aluminum foil and an empty bottle of Patron sat on the nightstand.

I laughed insanely as Mario gesticulated wildly, dictating his crazy tirade out like a faux PSA announcement, "Tweekers? Let me tell you a thing or two about fucking tweekers, *cabron*. First, they begin by snorting lines, then smoking, eventually, they graduate to 'slamming' using needles. Your basic meth addict will kill and die for their dope and can never be cured! They'll want it every day for the rest of their lives! They never want to see anyone unless they're tweeking. They are afraid of everything, except death. All of their friends are goddamn parolees which means they 'ain't shit' until they've been to prison at least once. They steal everything in sight, draw sexually explicit pictures, talk shit, get the lamest tattoos, disappear for days or even weeks in masturbation marathons, will physically assault the people they love, and slash their fucking wrists and arms. They will lose up to 100 pounds in a few days. They will spend all their money and lose any job they might've once had - fucking tweekers are unemployable, anyway. They hate themselves and everyone around them. They will spend 5 to 40 hours straight beating off and sticking things up their asses. Some will even steal panties from apartment dryers and wear them. They got no damn shame! Fucking tweekers will eventually accomplish self fellatio once they put their mind to it! *Si, si, senor!* I'm telling you; *anything* is possible when you're on speed!" He rolled on top of me, pointing straight at my face, "On speed, *guero*, the world belongs to *you.*"

It was funny at the time. Too bad it all came true. For both of us. We were simply too sick to realize it.

I grabbed the VCR and walked down to the corner café and waited through four coffees for the pawnshop to open. I sold the machine for one-hundred pesos.

By mid-afternoon, I was standing in the cavernous bus terminal of Tijuana. I purchased my one-way ticket to Ciudad Juárez, the city on the opposite side of the Rio Grande from El Paso, Texas.

Leaning against a large, white column, smoking, I waited for my exile eastward.

A flat, tinny voice squawked over the speakers in a language I didn't quite understand as groups of locals meandered about. A baby cried, a fat man in a red t-shirt that read *Happiness Is Coming!* stood in black, wraparound sunglasses, people languidly chewed gum, read magazines, or simply silently stared at everyone else.

Eventually, a fat steward announced it was time to board our bus. I filed on with the other passengers - mostly elderly. I stored my bag in an overhead compartment and hunkered down in a seat to myself and waited to be transported into the unknown.

With a squealing of gears and a fart of black exhaust, the mighty bus pulled from the station. I stared out the grimy window - saddened and bitter. Yet, I had no regrets about leaving a place in which no one would care I was gone.

I began my trek east, realizing from here on out, I was a marked man and must keep on my guard. I become aware of my ravaged reflection in the window. Tired, paranoid eyes gazed back at me and I admitted to myself repeating the words of Ismael, I did look truly lost...

Tijuana, 1994

AUTHOR'S BIO

Born in the Deep South to a lower-upper-middle class family, Luis Blasini was raised in Los Angeles, California as an ardent fan of the arts. Attending film school and majoring in English Literature at a Southern California University – the Author was influenced by avant-garde film directors and well-read in the written works of the Beat Generation. He graduated with honors in both Cinema Direction and Literature.

Uninterested by the plastic lifestyle of Los Angeles, he relocated to the slums of Tijuana, Mexico where - integrating with the local junkies, thieves, male hustlers, and notorious expat homosexuals of Zona Norte - the Author continued to keep detailed journals of a deliciously degenerate lifestyle among the back alleys of the border slums.

Going on a 'Kerouac Kick', he fled Tijuana and for a decade wandered aimlessly as a self-proclaimed 'hobosexual' – the Author traveled and explored the span of the United States,

Caribbean, Central and South Americas. All the while, recording his outrageous, yet intriguing experiences in a world renowned blog.

To learn more about the author,
enjoy his blog at:
www.borrowedflesh.blogspot.com

Made in the USA
Las Vegas, NV
10 April 2023

70432395R00134